ACCESS 2000

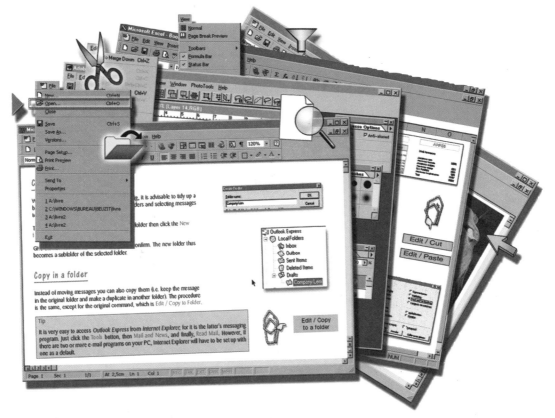

Jean-Paul MESTERS

The author explains the best way to use each command. You gain from that professional's experience of constantly looking for the best way to use the software, ie. the fastest and simplest. But that's not all! Understanding a command is one thing; understanding how it can be used is another. These two aspects are both covered in the explanations provided.

Often a command can be or must be combined with another command in order to achieve a desired result. The relations between commands are of several kinds: combination, complement, extension, etc. Understanding the links between commands is a guarantee of success. The link to another command is given at the bottom of the page in the form of a string such as: Menu/ Command/Options or Subcommand.

The 'shortcut keys' are combinations of keystrokes that let you execute a command quickly without using your mouse. You are well advised to memorise the shortcuts for the commands you use a lot, because the repetitive movement of the mouse in order to pull down menus and click on commands is tiresome. Not only will you save

quite a bit of time but you will also gain confidence as a user. Whenever a command has a shortcut key, we note it.

Occasionally, a Toolbar button provides another quick way to execute a command. In such cases it is given along with the shortcut key. It's a nice compromise between the shortcut key and a menu. It's easier to remember a picture than a string of letters.

A 'paperclip' guide will appear every time the author has something special to say or a tip to give you. This paperclip indicates that the relevant command contains an additional explanation. It is either a related command or a particularly useful option of the command described.

ABOUT FULL SCREEN

The Full Screen series aims to provide a new way of presenting books on software. By flipping quickly through this book, you will have already realised this. You will have gone through a list of menu items identical to those within the program. On the left, the command menu scrolls up and down. All that's missing is the sound of mouse clicks to make you think you're sitting in front of your PC or Mac screen. Since we could not include this characteristic little noise, we have instead highlighted each command.

Except for this detail, your Full Screen book reflects precisely the environment in which you are likely to be working. You are using the very first WYSIWYG (*What You See Is What You Get*) book. With MS Windows used in both home and office settings for some 15 years now, it is high time that the book adapted to most computer users' way of experiencing things.

A new type of book requires a new way of reading. The Full Screen series has been created to meet the specific needs of users of software programs. The book and the program go hand in hand; they move in the same direction. When you encounter a problem, you don't waste time leafing through the book in search of an explanation for a particular command, dialogue box or option. The explanations, suggestions and the tips are found in the book in the same places where the command is found in the program. Conversely, you can move just as easily from the book to the screen.

The books in the Full Screen series are intended for beginners. They do not cover all the commands of a software package, because this would make the book unnecessarily complicated (since in some cases there are several hundreds of such commands!). Through these books you will learn to use the forty or so commands that lie at the heart of each program, the ones that let you use it on a daily basis either in a professional setting or at home.

Reports are used for printing and analysing the data from tables directly or through queries. They can be used to organise fields and lay them out on the printed page; they can also do calculations (e.g. calculate the stock value for each article). Furthermore, they can be used to carry out statistical calculations and group data by categories (e.g. a list of customers town by town).

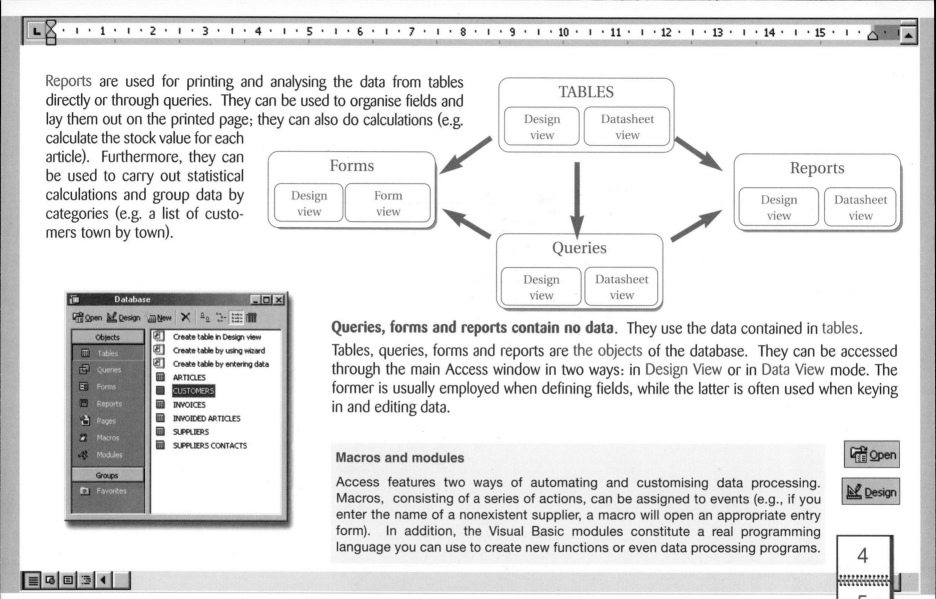

Queries, forms and reports contain no data. They use the data contained in tables.

Tables, queries, forms and reports are the objects of the database. They can be accessed through the main Access window in two ways: in Design View or in Data View mode. The former is usually employed when defining fields, while the latter is often used when keying in and editing data.

Macros and modules

Access features two ways of automating and customising data processing. Macros, consisting of a series of actions, can be assigned to events (e.g., if you enter the name of a nonexistent supplier, a macro will open an appropriate entry form). In addition, the Visual Basic modules constitute a real programming language you can use to create new functions or even data processing programs.

What is a database ?

A database contains a set of data as well as the means for reading, filtering, organising, processing and presenting it.

The data is stored in tables, and all the data in a table pertains to a specific subject (e.g. the articles sold in a shop or the customers of that business). In such a table, each row contains all the data relating to each article, while each column represents a specific piece of information: the name of the article or the price for example. In database jargon, a row is called a record and a column a field.

Queries allow you to customise and filter the data. For example, a query could display only the name and the price of articles of which there are more than 10 units in stock. Furthermore, queries can act on the data. For example, you can use the queries to display the price of articles inclusive of all tax, increase the price of all articles by 10%, or delete all articles over six months old.

Forms present data from tables in datasheet or table form, filtered when necessary by a query. The form window can be used to view, add or update table data; it can also be used to automate certain actions (e.g. to show data after having carried out statistical calculations).

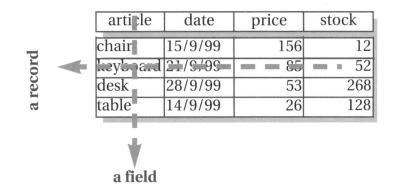

a record

article	date	price	stock
chair	15/9/99	156	12
keyboard	21/9/99	85	52
desk	28/9/99	53	268
table	14/9/99	26	128

a field

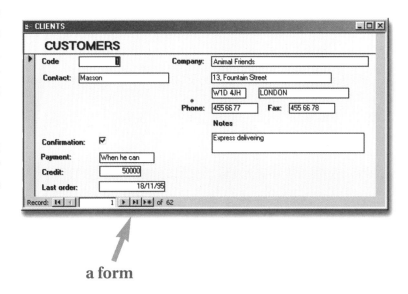

a form

Interlinked tables

A database usually contains several interlinked tables. To link the tables, each record must have a unique identifier (a field containing a data item that can identify each record uniquely). Furthermore, a common field must be provided in the two tables to establish the relationship.

For example, the Articles table contains a list of articles for sale and the Suppliers table contains a list of companies that supply the articles. In the Suppliers table, each record is identified by a sequence number (in the number field). In the Articles table, each record is identified by a single code, and a field is reserved for the supplier number (suppl number). It will be used to establish the relationship with the Suppliers table. The link fields are therefore *suppl* (in the Articles table) and *number* (in the Suppliers table).

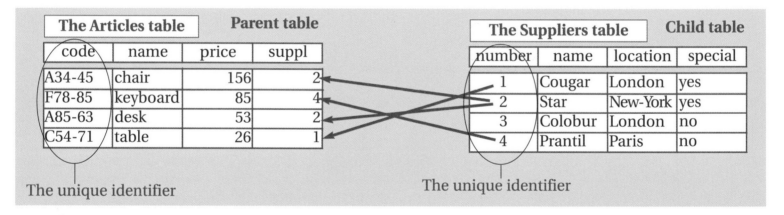

A record in the Suppliers table is linked with several records in the Articles table in what is known as a *one-to-many* relationship. The table on the 'one' side is the parent in the relationship, while the table on the 'many' side is the child. See pages 84-85 for information on how to create relationships between tables.

Relational databases in *Access* must always comply with this model. The example on pages 8-9 shows how they work.

Relational databases: five rules

A relational database must meet very precise criteria, otherwise it could become unusable when you try to update it by adding fields or tables. The basic rule is that a piece of information must be located in one place only. In practice, this means the same piece of data must not be contained in two different fields, nor in two different tables.

When you create tables, follow these five instructions:

❶ One piece of data per field: e.g. put the surname and the first name in two different fields.

❷ No duplication of data: one piece of data must be in one field only (e.g. don't enter date of birth and age, as they actually represent the same data item, because the age can be calculated from the date of birth).

❸ Field independence: the modification of the contents of a field must not force you to modify another data item (e.g. if you have provided a field for the prices exclusive of tax, you must not have to provide a field for the price inclusive of all taxes).

❹ No calculation result in the fields: the fields would not be independent in such a case (e.g. the price inclusive of all tax is the result of a calculation carried out on the price exclusive of tax).

❺ A single index per table: this field is called the 'primary key'.

To create a relational database, define a table per area of information: e.g. one Customers table, one Articles table, one Suppliers table. Provide a common field in each of the tables to link: the unique identifier in the parent table and a link field in the child table. Avoid enumerative tables: for example Child1, Child2, Child3. Rather, create one table that contains all the fields of Child 1, Child 2, Child 3. See how the tables of the sample database are linked on the next page.

N.B.: In this book we refer to 'parent' and 'child', but *Access* refers to 'master' and 'child'. For the purposes of this book therefore 'parent' = 'master'.

Sample database

The Suppliers/Contacts table contains the following fields:

Code (unique identifier – primary key).

Supplier Code (unique identifier – primary key): serves as a link to the Suppliers table.

Last Name (text field).

First Name (text field).

Code	Supplier Code	Last Name	First Name
1	1	Smith	John
2	2	Ingham	François
3	3	Cartmell	Patrick
4	5	Hondel	Angela
5	4	Morris	Simone
6	2	Brown	Alice
7	1	Taylor	Eric
8	4	Ward	Roger
9		Collins	Bill
10	6	Lanter	Maria
11	7	Mooner	Stephen
12	8	Stables	George
13	10	Pell	Valy

SUPPLIERS CONTACTS : Table

Record: 1 of 14

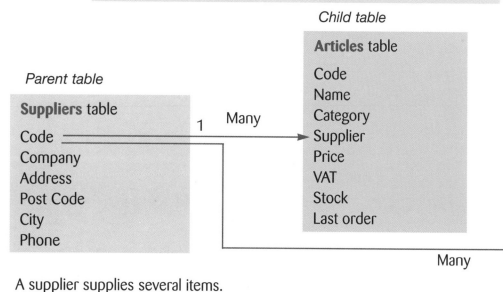

Child table

Articles table

Code
Name
Category
Supplier
Price
VAT
Stock
Last order

Parent table

Suppliers table

Code
Company
Address
Post Code
City
Phone

1   Many

Child table

Suppliers/Contacts table

Code
Supplier Code
Last Name
First Name

Many

A supplier supplies several items.

A supplier has several contacts.

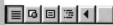

Sample database

When storing data, you must create one table for each type of information you wish to track. The examples pertain to the database of a shop for which three tables have been designed:

❶ **Articles table:** each record in this table contains the data of an article.

❷ **Suppliers table:** each record contains the data of a supplier.

❸ **Suppliers/Contacts table:** each record contains the data of a contact (all suppliers and other contacts).

The Articles table contains the following fields:

Code (unique identifier – primary key).
Name (text field): name of article.
Category (text field).
Supplier (number field): serves as a link to the Suppliers table.
Price (number field).
VAT (number field).
Stock (number field).
Last order (number field).

ARTICLES : Table

Code	Name	Category	Supplier	Price	VAT	Stock	Last order
05-303	Guest chair	Furniture	7	40	20,6%	55	05/09/99
07-390	Round Table	Furniture	8	61	20,6%	19	05/09/99
08-151	Half-height unit	Furniture	1	134	20,6%	8	05/09/99
09-077	Low sectional unit	Furniture	1	48	20,6%	16	05/09/99
11-518	Executive desk	Furniture	1	107	20,6%	18	05/09/99
11-543	Large desk	Furniture	3	67	20,6%	4	05/09/99
11-573	Secretarial desk	Furniture	1	97	20,6%	24	05/09/99
11-583	Small desk	Furniture	1	63	20,6%	18	05/09/99
14-040	Mobile three-drawer filing cabinet	Furniture	1	81	20,6%	3	05/09/99
15-991	Printer stand	Furniture	9	46	20,6%	41	08/09/99

Record: 9 of 41

The Suppliers table contains the following fields:

Code (unique identifier – primary key).
Company (text field).
Address (text field).
Post Code (text field).
City (text field).
Phone (text field).

SUPPLIERS : Table

Co	Company	Address	Post Code	City	Phone
1	Buro	121 South Molton Street	W1Y 1HY	London	0171 225 5665
2	RapidService	128 East Street	PO16 9XE	Portchester	0185 552 236
3	XLStore	4 Stroud Road	GL1 4JE	Gloucester	01452 541 499
4	Center Red	15 Blackwater Church Road	E4F 2JH	London	0170 256 2232
5	Alpha plus	17 Picpus Street	MA2 9JB	Manchester	02364 521 578
6	Martin Company	4523 Blalock Road	N5K 8LP	London	0171 552 6336
7	Enterprise Edition	7 Smith Brewer Road	MA2 3BF	Manchester	02364 587 451
8	Audio Max	108 Pearl Street	CA3 8AC	Canterbury	07852 569 324
9	Info Media	5 Houser Road	W3G 5GC	London	0172 225639 47
10	Modern Style	885 Station Street	MA5 7CD	Manchester	02365 552 668

Record: 1 of 10

Name a database

Since *Microsoft Office* provides the My Documents folder, why not use it? You can put all your documents and all your databases in it.

Click in the left bar on the My Documents icon: the window will display the contents of this folder.

Double-click the icon of the subfolder in which you want to save your database. If necessary, create a subfolder by clicking the Create folder button.

Enter the name of the file in the File name field and click the Create button. Note that *Access* database files have the extension .mdb.

File names can comprise any characters (including space), except for \ ? : " < and >.

Create new folder

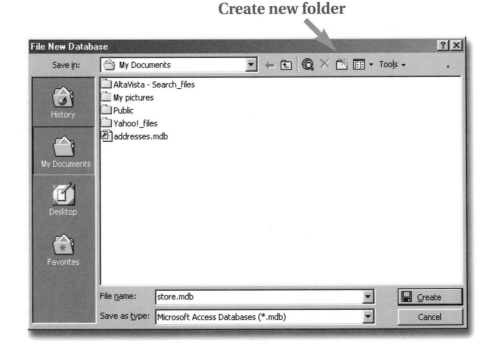

Insert/Table

10

Create a database

To start a new database you must select a template for it. Click File/New, and a dialogue window will suggest several templates.

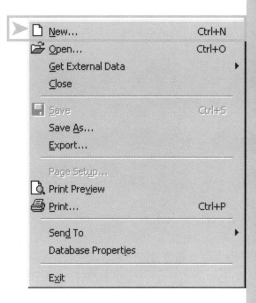

To start from scratch (i.e. with a blank database), select the General tab, then the template called Database and click OK. You can then create the tables and different objects necessary.

In the Databases tab, *Access* features nine Wizards. These will help you to create specific databases by offering tables, forms, reports and a start menu.

File/New

Contrary to a word-processing program, where you do not have to save a new document immediately, you must give a name to a database, because every new piece of data and every modification of a data item is saved immediately and automatically in the file.

Open a database

You can also open a database directly from Windows Explorer or from a Desktop folder. Double-click the icon of the *Access* file to open it.

When you open *Access*, an initial dialogue box appears automatically. From this window, you can create a blank database from scratch, use a Wizard or open an existing file. If you choose More files, you open the standard dialogue box. Otherwise, you can select the name of a previously opened database from the list.

When you choose File/Close, the open database is closed. As the data is saved automatically, *Access* does not ask you (as *Word* does, for example) to confirm. That is also why the Save command in the File menu is not available.

Forms, queries and reports must be saved after they are created and after every modification.

File/Close

12

13

Database

Open a database

Access can manage only one database at a time. If a database is already open, it will be closed automatically when you open another one. But you can always run Access several times, which will enable you to open a different database in each window.

In the dialogue box, select the folder containing the database file. Now select the file you want to open and then click the Open button.

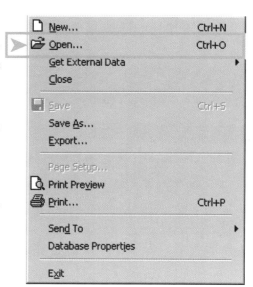

When you click the Tools button in the upper part of the dialogue box, then the Find command, you can search on your hard disk for a database whose location you have forgotten.

It is not always necessary to select the Open command. In fact, the names of the last four databases opened are indicated at the bottom of the File menu. Click the one you want.

File/Open

Print preview

Only visible data will be printed as it appears in the window on the screen. For example, if you print a datasheet, only the visible columns and records will appear on the paper.

To avoid wasting time and paper, preview the document as it will be printed by using the File/Print Preview command.

On the Toolbar, the magnifier (zoom) button is used to zoom on the page, while the next three display one, two or three pages simultaneously. You can print directly from this window (use the File/Print command or the print button). Finally, the Close button shuts down the preview window.

If you prefer to send data by email, it is very simple. In the File menu, select the Send to command, then Mail recipient and then one of the formats proposed: *Rich Text Format* (to send in word processing format), *Microsoft Excel* or *HTML* (to obtain a file that can be read in an Internet browser).

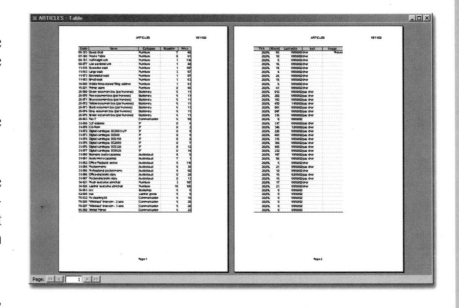

File/Print
Preview

Access: File/Print

Print the data

Although reports are specially designed for printing, you can always print the datasheet (showing the contents of a table or the result of a query) or layout data in a form.

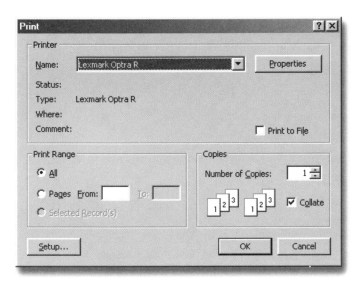

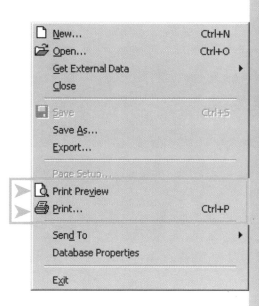

In the main window, select the object to be printed and then the File/Print command.

Enter the number of copies and indicate, if necessary, the pages to be printed. Sorted copies will take longer to print, but you will be spared the effort of having to resequence the pages afterwards.

Click the Setup button to open a new dialogue box containing one or two tabs depending on the type of object you want to print: for tables and queries, the Margins tab only will appear; for forms and reports, the Margins and Columns tabs will appear. The latter enables you to arrange the data in columns. Make sure that the margins are large enough: 10mm minimum for each.

File/Print

With the File/Page Setup command (available only for forms and reports), you will have access to a third tab, Page, in which you can determine the orientation and size of the paper.

Grouping objects

Click on an object with the right mouse button to open a shortcut menu with a few extra commands in addition to those in the Edit menu.

By default, the objects are grouped by type (tables, forms, etc.), but you can put them in customised groups. For example, one group for objects required for consulting, another for encoding data, etc. Click one of the objects with the right mouse button. The Add To Group command invites you either to create a new group, or to place a shortcut of the object in one of the existing groups. You can also move the object with the mouse on to the icon of one of the existing groups (in the left pane, under the Groups tab). To display the contents of a group, click its icon in the left pane.

The Create shortcut command will place a shortcut of the object in a *Windows* folder (Desktop, for example). Double-click this shortcut to open both the database and the object.

The Properties command gives you the opportunity to type a comment that will be visible in the Database window in Details View mode.

Insert/Table - Query
- Form - Report

16

17

Organising the database window

All the different database objects are grouped in the database window. To open an object in Datasheet View mode, double-click its icon. To open in Design View mode, double-click its icon while keeping the Ctrl key pressed.

To copy one of them, just copy it in the Clipboard (with the Edit/Copy command) and then paste it (with the Edit / Paste command). A small dialogue box will then ask you to name the new object, because *Access* will not allow two objects of the same type to have the same name. You can also drag the object with the mouse while keeping the Ctrl key pressed.

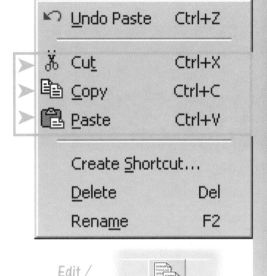

Edit /
Copy

Ctrl + C

To delete an object, select it and press the Del key (or use the Edit/Delete command). Warning: there is no recycle bin. The deletion is final.

To rename an object, press the F2 key or use the Edit/Rename command.

Edit /
Paste

You can always undo the last (but only the last) action by using the Edit/Undo command.

Ctrl + V

AutoNumber field

When you have created a new table, as you close the Create table window, *Access* checks that one of the fields has been defined as the primary key. If not, it offers to create one for you. It enters a new AutoNumber field that it names ID.

When you enter or modify data, *Access* will refuse any duplicates in the Primary Key field, something that could occur if the field is not an AutoNumber. If it is this data type, it will be automatically given a numeric value, attributed uniquely (definitively) to the record. When a record is deleted, for example, values already attributed are not changed so it is not a record number. To avoid any mistakes, this field is read-only: you cannot modify its contents.

Tools/Relationships

Access: Edit/Primary key

Primary key

Every database table must contain a single identifier or primary key. This is a field that will contain a unique piece of data for each record, e.g. a customer number or article code. This field is essential for establishing a relationship between the table and other tables in the database. It is called the primary key and will be either defined by you, or created automatically by *Access*.

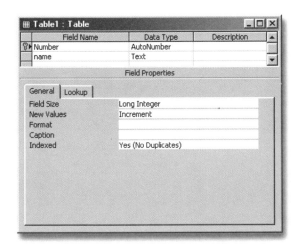

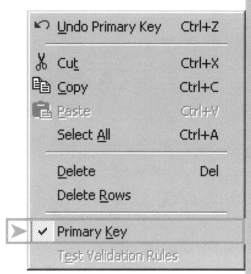

If you create the primary key yourself, enter the field that will serve as single identifier. The type of data does not matter (text, number or date). *Access* has provided a specific type of such field: AutoNumber. Every time you enter a new record, this field will be automatically incremented. For example, if the last record of the table contains the value 125 in this field, the next record will be given the value 126.

Now attribute the primary key to this field, either with the Edit/Primary Key command, or by clicking the Primary Key button. To cancel the primary key, click in the name of the field and use the same command.

Primary Key

Copy/Paste

When you paste entire fields, make sure that the field type of destination corresponds to that of the fields copied. You cannot, for example, enter letters in a number field by pasting. In case of error, *Access* displays the two error messages shown on the right. The second informs you that the incompatible data is not lost but transferred in a table created for that purpose called 'paste errors'.

To add new records by copying existing records, select them, then click the grey box in the column in front of the first field. Copy them to the Clipboard with the Edit/Copy command. Then paste with the Edit/Paste command.

APPLICATION

The value you entered isn't valid for this field.

For example, you may have entered text in a numeric field or a number that is larger than the FieldSize setting permits.

OK

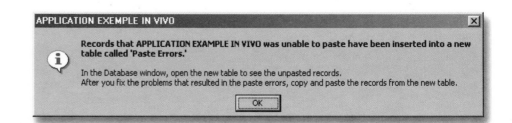

APPLICATION EXEMPLE IN VIVO

Records that APPLICATION EXAMPLE IN VIVO was unable to paste have been inserted into a new table called 'Paste Errors.'

In the Database window, open the new table to see the unpasted records.
After you fix the problems that resulted in the paste errors, copy and paste the records from the new table.

OK

Warning

If the primary key field is not an AutoNumber field, you will not be able to paste the records. Duplicates are prohibited in the primary key field since it is the single identifier of the records.

Edit/Replace

20

21

Copy, Cut and Paste

The Clipboard is available in *Access* as in the other *Microsoft Office* applications so you can copy, cut and then paste data elsewhere. But these three well-known commands function in two different ways: either on characters or on entire fields.

To select characters inside a field, click in the field (the cursor will turn into a black arrow, shown here on the right). Copy the selection to the Clipboard. Select the destination you want by clicking inside a field and use the Edit/Paste command to paste.

To select an entire field, point at the very beginning of the field (the cursor turns into a cross) and click (see the example on the right). Here, the field and its contents are placed in the Clipboard with the Edit/Copy command. Before you paste, select an area of fields of the same size as that in the Clipboard, and then paste. For example, if you have copied three rows and two columns, select three rows and two columns before you paste.

ARTICLES : Table

	Code	Name	Category
	05-303	Guest chair	Furniture
	07-390	Round Table	Furniture
	08-151	Half-height unit	Furniture
▶	09-077	Low **sectional** unit	Furniture
	11-518	Executive desk	Furniture
	11-543	Large desk	Furniture
	11-573	Secretarial desk	Furniture

Record: I◀ ◀ | 4 | ▶ ▶I ▶* of 41

ARTICLES : Table

	Code	Name	Category
	05-303	Guest chair	Furniture
	07-390	Round Table	Furniture
	08-151	Half-height unit	Furniture
▶	09-077	Low sectional unit	Furniture
	11-518	Executive desk	Furniture
	11-543	Large desk	Furniture
	11-573	Secretarial desk	Furniture

Record: I◀ ◀ | 4 | ▶ ▶I ▶* of 41

✂ Cut		Ctrl+X
🖹 Copy		Ctrl+C
📋 Paste		Ctrl+V
Paste Special...		
Paste as Hyperlink		
Paste Append		
Delete		Del
Delete Record		
Delete Column		
Select Record		
Select All Records		Ctrl+A
🔍 Find...		Ctrl+F
Replace...		Ctrl+H
Go To		▶

Cut   **Ctrl** + **x**

Ctrl + **c**   Copy

Paste   **Ctrl** + **v**

NUM

Wildcard characters

Three wildcard characters can be used in the Find What field:

❶ ? replaces any single character.

❷ # replaces a number.

❸ * replaces any number of characters.

For example, by searching with 'DU#12', Access will find 'DU512' but not 'DUA12'. By searching with 'ba??oon', Access will find 'balloon' but not 'battalion'. On the other hand, with 'ba*on', both 'balloon' and 'battalion' will be found.

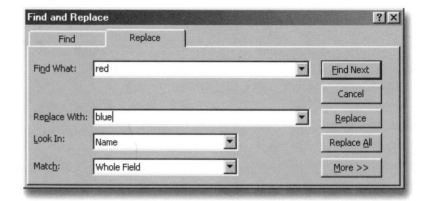

Access will continue to search as long as you keep clicking the Find Next button. To hide the bulky dialogue box, conduct an initial search and then close it by clicking on the Cancel button. The Shift + F3 key combination is then equivalent to the Next button.

The settings of the replace procedure are the same. The Find Next button searches for the next data item. The Replace button replaces the item found and the Replace All button replaces all the data without stopping on each item.

Edit/Copy

22

23

Find and Replace

To find a specific entry in a table, start by clicking in the record from which the search is to be carried out. If necessary, click in the field in which the data item is located.

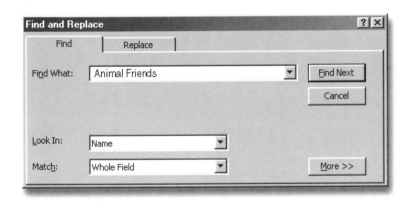

Select the Edit/Find command. Enter the data you want to find in the Find What field. In the Look In field, you can choose between the selected field and the entire table.

In the Match list, select the place where the item you want to find is located: Whole Field, Any Part of Field, Start of Field. Click the Find Next button. *Access* will select the data item where it finds it in the datasheet.

For example, you want to find a record that has a field containing the data 'Animal Friends', you enter in the Find What field 'Friends'. If you have chosen the Any Part of Field option, *Access* will find this data. If, however, you have chosen one of the other two options, the data will not be found. If you type 'Animal', *Access* will find it with either the Any Part of Field or Start of Field match options, but will not find it with the Whole Field match option.

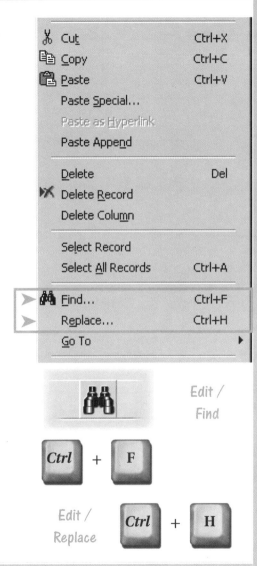

Navigation keys

When you use the scroll arrows or the Tab key, you select the next or previous entire field. As soon as you press a key on the keyboard, the item of data is immediately replaced by the character you typed. To obtain a normal text cursor, press F2. Press F2 again for field-by-field navigation.

The way the keyboard functions is defined by default, but you can change it. Select the Tools/Options command and click on the Keyboard tab. The choices in the Move after Enter box provide three options for the Enter key: Don't move, Next Field and Next Record. The choices in the Behavior entering field box allow you to set what happens when you click in a field: Select entire field, Go to start of field, Go to end of field. The two choices in the Arrow key behavior box let you control how arrow keys move the cursor (into the next field or onto the next character). Finally the Cursor stops at first/last field checkbox and lets you decide whether to keep the cursor, when resting in the last field, from going on to the next record.

Edit/Find

ARTICLES : Table

Code	Name	Category	Supplier	Price
05-303	Guest chair	Furniture	7	40
07-390	Round Table	Furniture	8	61
08-151	Half-height unit	Furniture	1	134
09-077	Low sectional unit	Furniture	1	48
11-518	Executive desk	Furniture	1	107
11-543	Large desk	Furniture	3	67
11-573	Secretarial desk	Furniture	1	97

Record: 5 of 41

ARTICLES : Table

Code	Name	Category	Supplier	Price
05-303	Guest chair	Furniture	7	40
07-390	Round Table	Furniture	8	61
08-151	Half-height unit	Furniture	1	134
09-077	Low sectional unit	Furniture	1	48
11-518	Executive desk	Furniture	1	107
11-543	Large desk	Furniture	3	67
11-573	Secretarial desk	Furniture	1	97

Record: 5 of 41

Access: Edit/Go to

Navigating

The mouse can be used to move in a table using the scroll bars.

You can go to the first or the last record immediately with the Edit/Go To command. If you choose New Record, the pointer enables the empty record at the very bottom of the table (the one that displays an asterisk in the far left column). In the lower left corner of the window, you will find the fast navigation buttons along with the number of the record currently indicated. To move the pointer to a specific record, click in the blank field and enter the record number you want. Then press Enter.

You will save time if you use keyboard shortcuts.

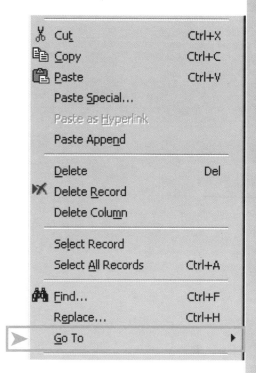

To go to:
- ➱ the first field of the first record: Ctrl+Home.
- ➱ the last field of the last record: Ctrl+End.
- ➱ the first field of the current record: Home.
- ➱ the last field of the current record: End.
- ➱ the next field: Right arrow or Tab.
- ➱ the previous field: Left arrow or Shift+Tab.

Special features for viewing objects

In List and Details modes, unlike in Small Icons, you cannot put the icons in the window as you want. They are lined up automatically and organised by name, type or date on which they were created or modified, according to your choice in the Arrange Icons command.

If the AutoArrange option at the bottom of the Arrange Icons list is enabled, the icons will be lined up automatically in Large Icons and Small Icons modes.

In Details mode, you cannot move the panes but you can change their relative widths. Place the cursor on the border between the panes. When the cursor turns into a double arrow, click and drag to the left or right. Furthermore, if you click on a title label (in the left-hand pane) you will expose the contents under that title. Click a second time to reverse that action.

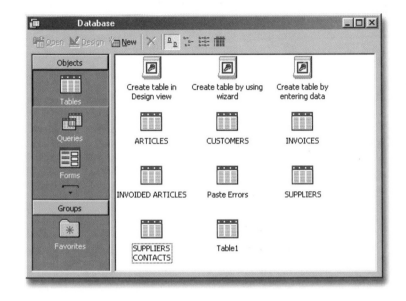

Refresh the display

The View/Refresh command updates (refreshes) the list of objects and the information relating to them.

Edit/Cut, Copy and Paste

Access: View/Icons, List and Details

Database

View database objects

In the left pane headed Objects, click on the type of objects you wish to view. All the selected objects in the database will be displayed on the right.

The settings of the View Database Objects command are the same as in a *Windows* folder screen. The View menu offers four standard ways of displaying the objects.

At the top of the Database window, you will recognise the four buttons corresponding to the view modes. Large Icons and Small Icons pertain to the left and right panes of the window.

Note that by choosing a type of object from View/Database Objects, you obtain the same result as when you click on one of the icons in the left window pane. The Arrange Icons and Line Up Icons commands arrange the objects and line them up in the window. Details displays the date the object was created and last modified as well as your comments (entered with the Properties command).

Field properties

A field name may contain a maximum of any 64 characters, including spaces, but not the following four characters: ! . [ ].

The number of fields is limited to 255 per table.

For each field, you must indicate the type of data it is to hold:

Text: Characters (letters, numbers, punctuation marks), up to a maximum of 255 characters per field.

Memo: Any characters, limited to 32 000 per field.

Number: Numbers.

Currency: Numbers automatically given the currency symbol.

Date/Time: Date and time.

Yes/No: The TRUE (YES) or FALSE (NO) value.

Hyperlink: A link to an Internet address or a file on your hard drive.

OLE: An OLE object (e.g. an image, an Excel spreadsheet, a Word document).

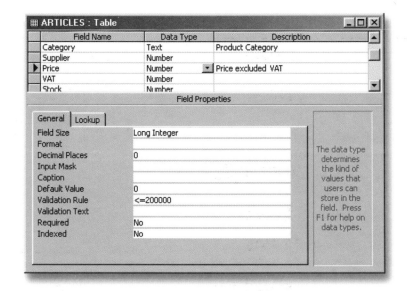

Insert/Table

28

29

Table structure

The table design screen opens when you choose to create a table in Design View or when you select an existing table and click the Design button.

The Design View window is divided into two panes. The upper pane is for the names of the fields (one per row) and the data type; the lower pane is for the field properties.

To define a field, enter its name in the first column, and select the data type from the list in the second column. For a text field, enter the maximum number of characters for it in the Field Size (in the lower pane).

To delete a field, use the Edit/Delete rows command.

To insert a field, use Insert/Rows.

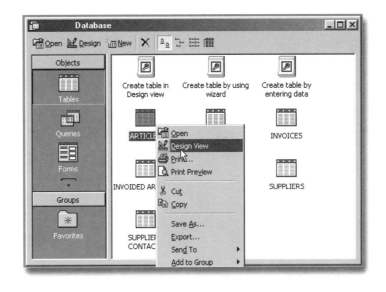

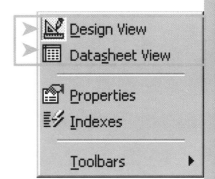

View/
Datasheet View

View/
Design View

When you have finished, close the window or switch to Datasheet View (to display the contents of the table) by clicking the View button in the upper left corner of the screen. *Access* will suggest that you save the changes; click Yes.

Add and delete records

 To add a record, click the New Record button. New records are always added at the bottom of the table.

To delete records, you must select them first: click the small box to the left of the first record you want to delete. Keep the button pressed and drag the mouse down until you have selected all the records you want to delete. Bear in mind that it is impossible to select non adjacent records. When you have made your selection, click Delete Record on the toolbar. A message informs you that the records are going to be deleted. Click the Yes button.

Warning: a deletion is always final. It will be impossible to recover the deleted records afterwards.

In closing the Datasheet window, *Access* will not ask you to save the data, because it is saved as it is written.

If you have modified the format of the sheet (the width of a column, for example), a message will ask you to save this new layout.

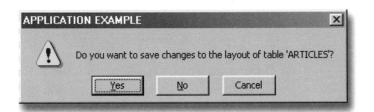

Format/Row Height -
Column Width

Access: View/Design and Datasheet views

Datasheet

Data

In Datasheet View, you have access to all the data of a table: to access a record, double-click the name of the table in the database window.

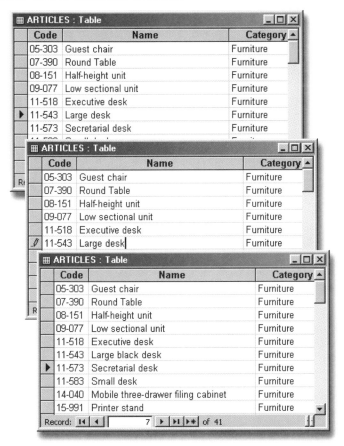

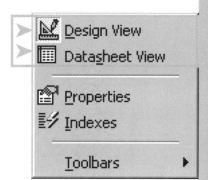

To modify a record, click in one of its fields to activate it first. The small arrow to the left of the record indicates that it is selected.

As soon as you modify a data item, a pencil is displayed in the place of the arrow. It informs you that the data displayed on the screen is no longer the same as that on the hard disk. When you click in another record, the data of the record you leave is saved immediately.

As long as you do not leave a record, you can cancel the changes you have made to it. Press the Esc key to restore the original data of the current field. Press Esc a second time to select the entire record: the changes to all the fields will subsequently be cancelled.

View /
Datasheet View

Select the fields you wish to view by clicking a field in the small window of the table and dragging it into the grid of the lower pane. To include all the fields, use the asterisk.

To move a field, select the column (point above the column and click when the cursor turns into a black arrow). Now click the grey bar just above the name of the field and drag it horizontally.

To delete a column, select it and press the Del key.

Test the effect of the query by selecting View/ Datasheet View. When the query is finished, save it and close its window. To retrieve it, click the Queries button on the left in the Database window, then double-click the query name to view the result.

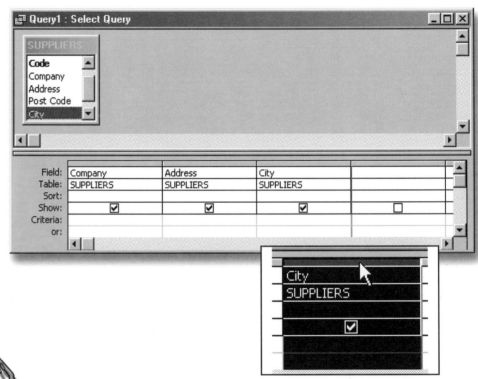

Insert/Queries

Create a query

There are two types of queries: select queries and action queries. Select queries displays the data of the tables without modifying it, whereas action queries automatically modifies the data to create a new table and, modifies the contents of a table or deletes records.

By default, a new query is a selection query in which you can:

- ⇒ link several tables;
- ⇒ select the fields to view;
- ⇒ filter and sort records;
- ⇒ carry out calculations on the data in the fields.

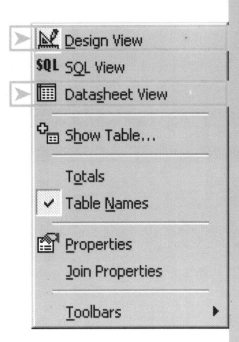

The Query Design screen opens when you opt to create a query in Design View or when you select an existing query and then click the Design button. For a new query, a dialogue box displays the list of tables: select the one for which you wish to create a query from and click the Add button.

The lower window pane is used to enter the query settings.

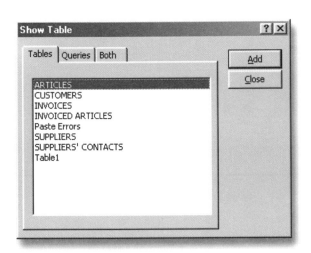

View/Datasheet View

View/Design View

View the data of the two tables

Drag the fields that you require into the grid of the lower pane in the order you prefer, regardless of the table of origin. The Table row in the grid displays the name of the tables. If required, enter the filter criteria.

In the datasheet view the records of the two tables for which the contents of the linked fields coincide will be displayed.

In our example, a row is displayed each time the Supplier field of the Articles table and the Number field of the Suppliers table have the same contents (i.e. are linked). Suppliers without articles and articles without suppliers are not displayed.

In the example opposite, the first three fields come from the Articles table and the fourth from the Suppliers table.

You can modify all the data in the datasheet. Only the contents of the primary key cannot be modified.

Query1 : Select Query

Name	Supplier	Company	Price
Guest chair	7	Enterprise Edition	40
Round Table	8	Audio Max	61
Half-height unit	1	Buro	134
Low sectional unit	1	Buro	48
Executive desk	1	Buro	107
Large black desk	3	XLStore	67
Secretarial desk	1	Buro	97
Small desk	1	Buro	63
Mobile three-drawer filing cabinet	1	Buro	81
Printer stand	9	Info Media	46
Green document box (per hundred)	5	Alpha plus	11
Red document box (per hundred)	5	Alpha plus	11
Blue document box (per hundred)	5	Alpha plus	11
Yellow document box (per hundred)	5	Alpha plus	11
Black document box (per hundred)	5	Alpha plus	11
Grey document box (per hundred)	5	Alpha plus	11
Brown document box (per hundred)	5	Alpha plus	11
3.5" diskette	9	Info Media	2
CD-Rom	9	Info Media	2
Digital cartridges DC300 XL/P	9	Info Media	8
Digital cartridges DC600	9	Info Media	8
Digital cartridges DC6150	9	Info Media	9
Digital cartridges DC2000	9	Info Media	7
Digital cartridges DC6320	9	Info Media	12
Digital cartridges DC6525	9	Info Media	14

Record: I◄ ◄ 12 ► ►I ►* of 41

Tools/Relationships

Access: View/Show table

34

35

| | | | | | | | | | | | | | | | | All ▾ | | | | | | | | | Query design |

Linking tables

A query may be based on several interlinked tables. In such a case, the data of each of the tables will be displayed in the datasheet.

To add a table in a query, use the View/Show Table command. Select the table in the list and click the Add button.

If you have created a relationship between the two tables previously (using the Tools/Relationships commands), it will be displayed immediately. If the two tables are not related, it is up to you to establish the relationship between them. Click on the parent table of the primary key (it appears in boldface characters). Keep the mouse button pressed and drag it on to the field you wish to link it to in the child table. For more details on the relationships between tables, see the introduction.

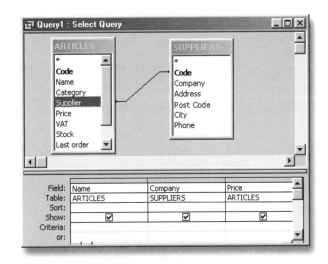

You can move the small windows of the tables by dragging them by their titles. To delete a table, click its name and press the Del key.

Design View
SQL SQL View
Datasheet View

▶ Show Table...

Totals
✓ Table Names

Properties
Join Properties

Toolbars ▶

View/
Show Table

Ready   NUM

The Event tab contains a list of events that can be produced for the control. A macro or *Visual Basic* routine can be assigned to each event and run when that event occurs; for instance, a macro that calculates the VAT-inclusive price each time the content of the Price field is modified.

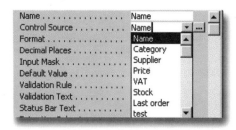

Click in the upper left corner of the form and its properties will appear in the Properties window.

In the Data tab, Source displays the name of the table or the query that the form is associated with. The other properties pertain to the functioning of the form. The Format tab contains the characteristics of the format and colours and also elements to present in the window (Close, Maximise and Minimise buttons, etc.).

Select the wallpaper by clicking on the small button to the right of the Image property.

Format/Autoformat

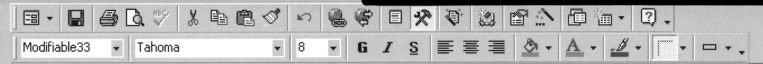

Form design

Modifiable33 ▾ | Tahoma ▾ | 8 ▾ | **G** *I* <u>S</u> | ≡ ≡ ≡ | ▨ ▾ | **A** ▾ | ✎ ▾ | ▭ ▾ | ▭ ▾

Control and form properties

Every control, as well as the form (or report) itself is defined by a series of characteristics known as properties. Some of them are accessed by the buttons of the formatting toolbar: font and font size, bold, etc. Just select the control, then click the button to apply the format.

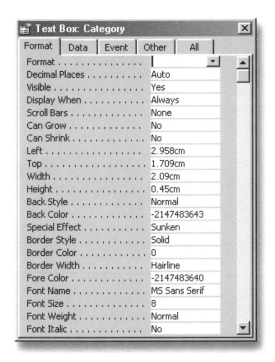

When you choose the View/Properties command, the Properties window appears. It displays the properties of the selected control. They are grouped by theme into five tabs.

For controls linked to a field of a table, the Format tab contains the properties corresponding to buttons of the formatting toolbar. In the Data tab, you will find, for example, Control Source, which contains the name of the field with which the control is associated. The Locked Property tab locks the field from any further update.

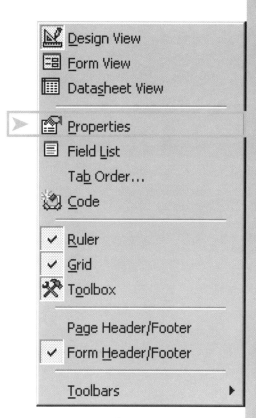

View / Properties

Design View | | | | NUM | |

Controls

Every element of the form is called a control. In the example on the right, the form has four controls. Two labels (in grey) and two text fields (in white). The text fields are linked to the fields of the table, whereas the labels contain free text. These controls are intercoupled: one label with one text field.

To select a control, click it. The handles (small squares) appear in the four corners and in the centre on each side.

To move both the intercoupled controls, click anywhere within the two controls and drag the mouse, whose point turns into a hand.

To move only one of the intercoupled controls, point to the larger square in its upper left corner. When the pointer turns into a hand at the desired point, click and drag with the mouse.

To change the size of a control point to one of the smaller handles. When the pointer turns into a double arrow, click and drag the mouse.

To delete a control: select it and press the Del key.

To test a form in Form mode, select View/Form View.

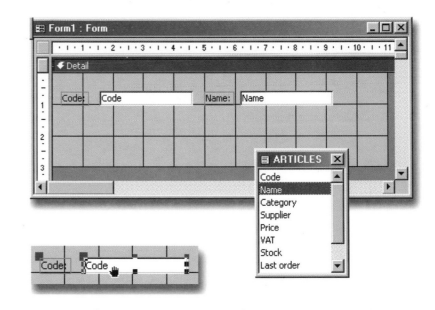

View/Field List

Access: View/Design View

Form design

Modifiable33 | Tahoma | 8 | **G** *I* S

Create a form or a report

The Form design window and Create report window are very similar: they feature the same commands and settings.

The Form (or Report) design window opens when you opt to create a form (or report) by clicking the New button in the Database window.

The same window opens when you select an existing form or report and then click the Design button. For a new form or report, a dialogue box is displayed: select from the list the table or the query that will supply the data and click OK.

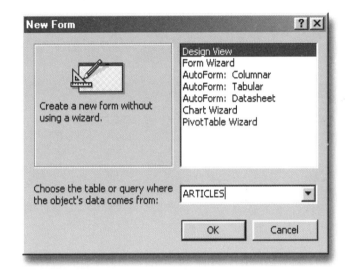

New Form

Create a new form without using a wizard.

Design View
Form Wizard
AutoForm: Columnar
AutoForm: Tabular
AutoForm: Datasheet
Chart Wizard
PivotTable Wizard

Choose the table or query where the object's data comes from: ARTICLES

OK   Cancel

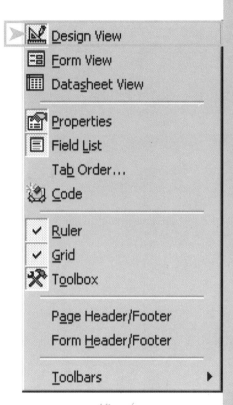

Design View
Form View
Datasheet View

Properties
Field List
Tab Order...
Code

✓ Ruler
✓ Grid
Toolbox

Page Header/Footer
Form Header/Footer

Toolbars ▶

View/
Design View

The button next to the form window opens the list of fields of the table selected in the previous step. The display of this list is controlled by the View/Field List command. Drag the names of the fields from this window into the form one by one. Not all the fields must be present in the form: the choice is up to you.

Print Preview

In the Print Preview window, you see the report as it will be printed. It is impossible to modify the data.

Navigate around the document using the buttons in the lower left corner of the window. You can view one, two or several pages on the screen and zoom up to 200%. The magnifying glass icon can be used to switch from zoom to displaying the page fitted to the size of the window. It can be activated by clicking the left button of the mouse.

Close the Preview window by clicking the Close button or print the document by clicking the Print button.

View/Form View

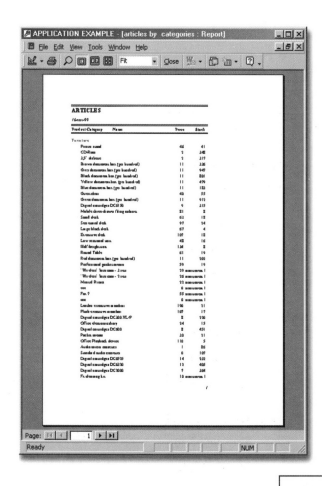

40

Modifiable33 | Tahoma | 8 | **G** *I* <u>S</u>

Use a form or a report

Double-click the icon of the form you wish to open in the Database window to open the form in Form View.

When you do the same with a report you open the Print Preview window. The information displayed by the forms and printed by the reports is constantly updated. In fact, neither the forms nor the reports contain data as such: they contain only layout, pre-view and formatting settings.

To navigate between records in a form, use the buttons in the lower left corner of the window.

Record: |◄| |◄| 12 |►| |►I| |►*| of 41

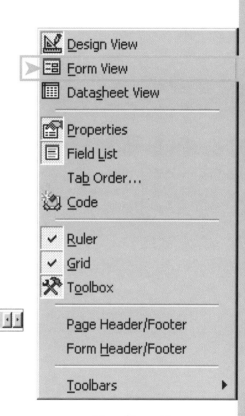

Warning

Every modification to the data is updated immediately in the table and will therefore be updated in the other objects linked to the same table.

Edit the data directly in the fields. To delete a record, click its selection button in the top left corner and press the Del key. To add a record, click the New Record button.

View/Form View

Design View | NUM

Lists

How do you insert a list box? First, the field must lend itself to such an operation: the list will contain a limited amount of data that can be entered into the field. The Category field in the Articles table is a good example, because the number of categories is limited. Make sure that the magic wand (Control Wizard) button is pressed.

Click the Combo Box in the Toolbox. Drag it into the form, then type the different values that will appear in the list 'information technology', 'furniture', 'stationery', etc.). Finally, confirm the choice by selecting from the dropdown list the desired field, Category.

To insert a line or a rectangle, click the button in the Toolbox and use the mouse to draw in the form.

If you lack space, resize the form by drawing its lower or left edge with the mouse.

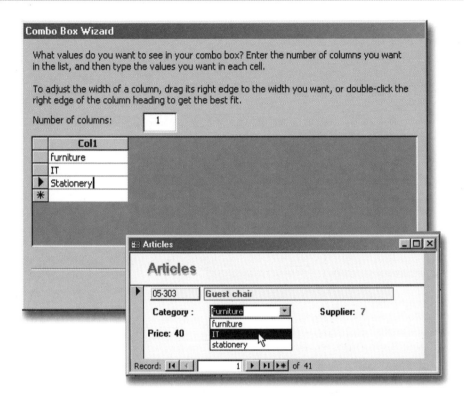

View/Field List

42

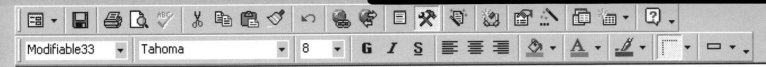

Form design

Controls

A form (or a report) is composed of controls. The Toolbox contains the different types of control: you can display it or close it with the View/Toolbox command. To find out the name of the controls just place the mouse (without clicking) on the different buttons of the Toolbox.

Some of them are linked to a field in the table: Text Box, Toggle Button, Option Button, Checkbox, Combo Box, List Box, Bound Object Frame, Subform. Others are independent: Label, Command Button, Image, Unbound Object Frame, Page Break, Line, Rectangle.

To insert a control linked to a field in the table on to the form, click in the Toolbox on the type of control you want to insert. Then select from the field list the name of the field you want to insert. Click in the form to position the control. If the field list is not displayed, choose the View/Field List command.

If the Control Wizard (magic wand) button is pressed in the Toolbox, you will be helped to set certain controls: Option Group, Combo Box, List Box and Command Button.

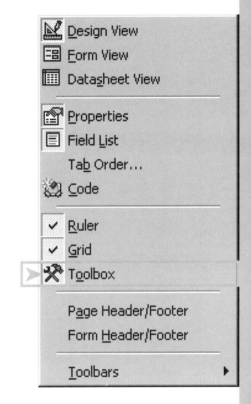

View/Toolbox

Design View

NUM

Insert a subform

From the main form, make sure that the magic wand (Control Wizard) button is pressed in the Toolbox. Click the Subform/Subreport button in the Toolbox. The Wizard starts: activate the Use existing form option and select the form you have just created from the list.

In the next step, select the name of the link field in the parent table (the primary key) from the first list: Number in our example. Click in the first list on the right and select the name of the joining field in the child table (Supplier). See the example on the right.

The subform is displayed. You can move it and resize it like any other control.

When you display the form in Form View, and scroll the different records of the Suppliers table, you will see the contents of the subform change and display the articles corresponding to each supplier.

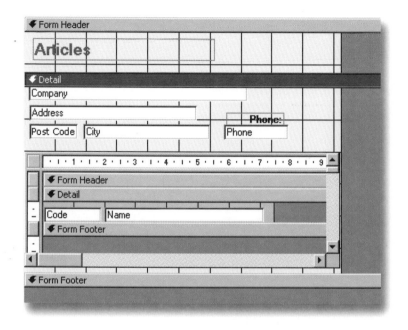

Tools/Relationships

Access: View/Toolbox

Subforms

A subform (or subreport) is used to display the data of two linked tables: the parent table in the main form and the child table in the subform. The two tables are linked by a common field (the primary key field in the parent table and a field of the same type in the child table).

To return to our example: a form could feature different suppliers and (in the subform) the articles that each one supplies.

Start by creating a form based on the child table (here the Articles table). Make sure that it is not too large so that a maximum number of records can be presented simultaneously. In the example to the right, it is composed of a single row of two fields and its default view was set on Continuous Forms in its format properties. Save it in the usual way. Then create the main form, based on the parent table (here the Suppliers table) and reserve a free space for the subform.

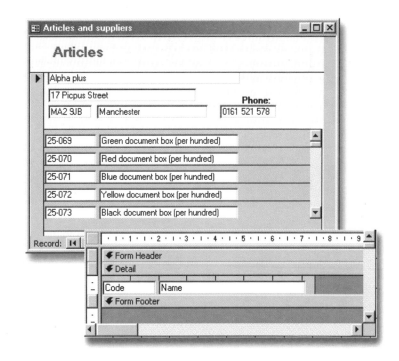

Design View

Section properties

The sections have properties that characterise their presentation and their functioning. Select the View/Properties command and click in an empty field inside a section.

Let us see some properties of a Detail section:

• **Force new page**: this section will always start on a new page.

• **Keep together**: this section will never be split into two different pages (unless it exceeds the height of a page).

• **Back colour**: click the small button on the right to select a colour in the palette. The choice is more varied than in the palette of the Back colour button in the Toolbar.

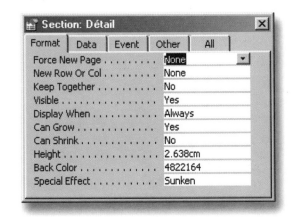

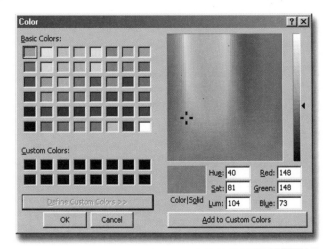

View/Page
Header and Footer

Access: View/Form Header and Footer

Form design

Sections

A form (or a report) is composed of five sections:

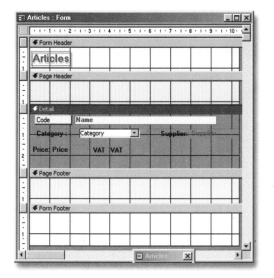

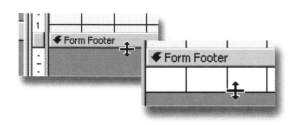

• **Detail**: presents the contents of the table and is repeated for each record.

• **Page header and page footer**: at the top and bottom of each page.

• **Form header and form footer**: remain fixed on the screen whereas the contents of the detail section can scroll.

To show or hide the sections, select the View/Page Header/Footer, View/Form Header/Footer. The sections are bound but you can always open or close each section individually by dragging its lower border.

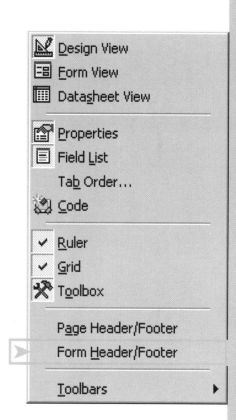

Design View

NUM

Create a table in Datasheet View

If you choose to create a table in Datasheet View, a window resembling a datasheet will open.

To name a field, double-click in the heading of the column and enter the name, making sure you observe the following rules:

• Do not exceed 64 characters.

• Use any character (including spaces) except the following signs: ! . [ ] .

• Limit yourself to 255 fields.

Once the fields have been named, you must define the type of data they will contain. Type in the first line a significant data example. For a text field, enter at least one letter. For a number field, type only numbers. For a date field, type a date in a form devoid of any ambiguity (e.g. "25/9/2000").

Now close the window. Enter the name you want to give to the new table. Finally, if you want to create a primary key, click Yes when asked.

View/Database objects/Table

48

49

Create a table

Access features three methods for creating a new table: Design View, Table Wizard and Datasheet View (opened with the Insert/Table command or in the Database window after clicking on the Tables button in the left pane).

The Wizard offers you a number of standard tables containing predefined fields. Start by selecting the type of table you want to create: Business or Personal. Then select a table from the Sample Tables list. In the Sample Fields list, click on the fields (one by one) that will compose your table and send them to the Fields in my new table box by clicking the right arrow button.

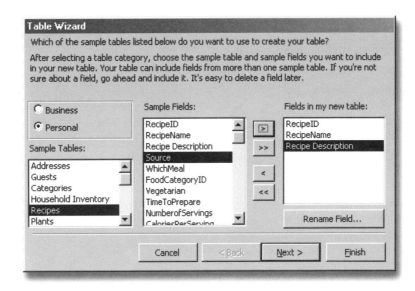

Click the Next button. Type the name you want to give to the table and select one of the two options concerning the primary key. For more details on the subject, see the Insert/Primary Key command. If this new table is related to another one, select it and click the Relationships button (the relationships are displayed in the Tools/Relationships window).

Table
Query
Form
Report
Page
Macro
Module
Class Module
AutoForm
AutoReport

Insert/Table

If you want a statistical summary, select in the first screen the text fields you want to group together and the number fields to which the statistical calculations will be applied: e.g. for the Articles table, choose the Category field, which will group the records and the price and stock fields for the statistical calculations.

In the next screen, select the Summary option and click the Summary Options button. Indicate the summary values you would like calculated for each number and finish creating the query.

Queries (detailed or summary) are saved automatically and displayed in the Database window. They don't contain data but instructions for processing the data of a table. Double-click the icon of a query in the Database window to apply the instructions it contains to the table to which it is associated.

For more details on the structure of queries, see the section on Query design mode (p. 32).

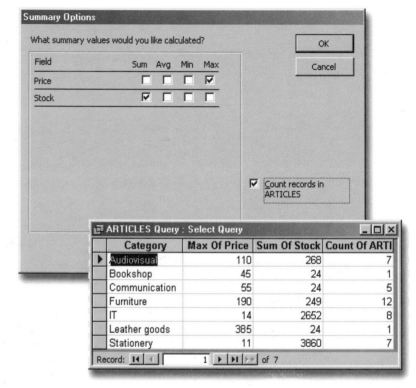

Category	Max Of Price	Sum Of Stock	Count Of ARTI
Audiovisual	110	268	7
Bookshop	45	24	1
Communication	55	24	5
Furniture	190	249	12
IT	14	2652	8
Leather goods	385	24	1
Stationery	11	3860	7

View/Database objects/Queries

50

Database

Create a query

Select queries helps you to use the data in tables. It enables you to select the fields you want to view and to filter records but does not change the data. Action queries, on the other hand, acts on the data by deleting records or editing data according to your instructions.

Access features two methods for creating a query: Design View and a Query Wizard. These two modes are available in the New Query dialogue box (opened with the Insert/Query command). They can also be accessed in the Database window once you have clicked the Queries button in the left pane.

The Simple Query Wizard helps you create a selection query. In the first screen, select the desired table(s) and/or queries from the drop-down list at the top of the window. The fields from the selected table or query will appear in the Available Fields box. Select the fields you want for your query by clicking the left arrow button. Fields from various tables or queries can be selected for one query. Click on Next after you have made your selection. In the next screen, leave the Detailed option activated and, finally, name the query and click Finish.

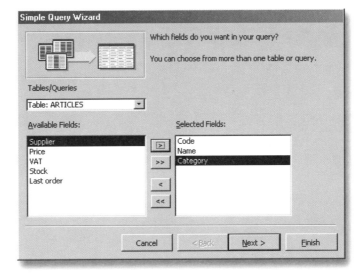

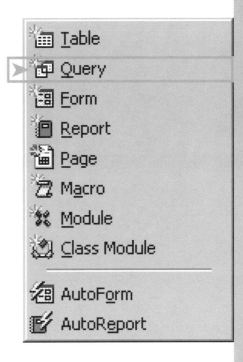

Insert/Query

AutoForms

In the New Form dialogue box, select one of the three AutoForms and select the table or the query to which the form will be applied. When you click OK, the form is created with all the fields of the table or the query selected and displayed for immediate use. When you close the form window, a message will suggest that you save it. If you want to keep it, click Yes and give it a name.

The result may not be perfect. You will often have to make some changes by opening the form in Design View.

Once saved, forms are displayed in the Database window. They contain no data but instructions on how to process the data of a table. Simply double-click the icon of a form in the Database window to apply the instructions and formatting it contains to the table to which it is associated.

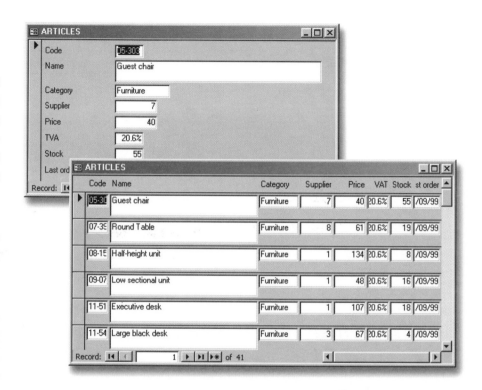

View/Database
objects/Forms

Access: Insert/Form

Database

Create a form

Forms present data of tables or queries in datasheet or table form.

Access features three ways of creating a form: Design View, three Wizards and three AutoForms. These three modes are available in the New Form dialogue box (opened with the Insert/ Form command). In the Database window, click the Forms button in the left pane to access the Wizards and the Design View.

The Form Wizard helps you create a simple form. In the first screen, select the table or query for which you want to create the form. Then select, one by one, the fields to view and move them from the Available Fields list to the Selected Fields list by clicking the right arrow button. In the next screen, select one of the four types of layout. Next, you must choose a graphics style. Finally, enter the name you want to give the form and click the Finish button.

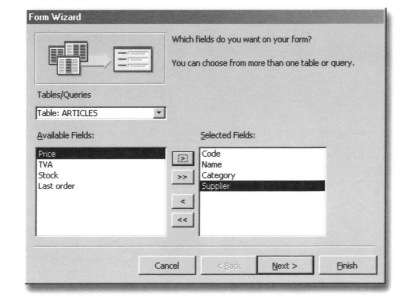

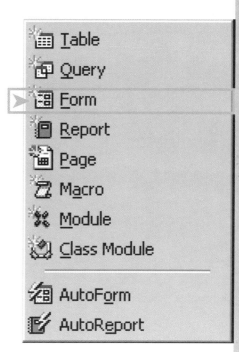

- Table
- Query
- **Form**
- Report
- Page
- Macro
- Module
- Class Module

- AutoForm
- AutoReport

Insert/Form

On the right is the result of the grouping by category and the sorting of the contents of the Heading field.

The Label Wizard will help you, step by step, to choose the label template and to arrange the fields.

The two AutoReports create a report rapidly with all the fields of the chosen table. In most cases, you will have to correct the layout in Design View.

As soon as the report is created, it is displayed in Print Preview. You can then print it by clicking the print button. When you click Close, the preview window closes. If you have created an AutoReport, *Access* will suggest that you save it. Click Yes and enter the name you want to give it.

The reports are in the Database window. They contain no data, only instructions for arranging it on the printed page. Double-click the icon of a report to have the instructions it contains applied to the table to which it is linked.

ARTICLES

Category	Code	Name	Supplier
Audiovisual			
	31-084	Pocket memo	8
	31-080	Standard audio cassettes	8
	31-082	Office Playback device	8
	31-085	Professional pocket memo	8
	31-086	Office electronic diary	9
	31-087	Pocket electronic diary	9
	31-081	Audio micro cassettes	7
Bookshop			
	35-663	ccc	5
Communication			
	78-997	"Wireless" Intercom - 3 sets	5
	25-663	Fax 7	5
	85-669	Minitel Printer	5
	78-996	"Wireless" Intercom - 2 sets	5
	75-632	Fx cleaning kit	5
Furniture			
	14-040	Mobile three-drawer filing cabinet	1
	11-583	Small desk	1
	11-573	Secretarial desk	1

View/Database/Objects/Report

Access: Insert/Report

Create a report

Reports print the data of tables or queries in table form. You must position the fields and choose the formatting.

Access features three ways to create a report: Design View, three Wizards and two AutoReports. These three methods are available in the New Report dialogue box (opened with the Insert/Report command). In the Database window, click on the Reports button in the left pane to access the Wizards and the Design View.

In the first screen of the Report Wizard, select the table or query for which you wish to create the report. Then select, one by one, the fields you want to print from the Available Fields list; when you have made your selection, click Next.

In the next screen, select the fields you want to group. For example, if you

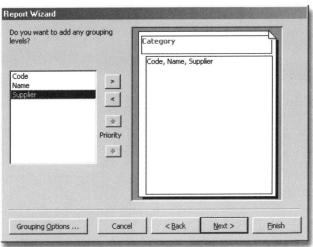

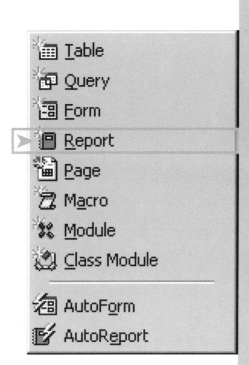

Insert/Report

Grouping levels

Grouping data by level makes it possible to carry out statistical calculations (sums, averages, etc.) on a level by level basis. In this example, the articles are grouped by category, so we will get the number of articles in each category.

select the Category field for the Articles table, the list of articles will be printed category by category. In the next screen, select the layout. Finally, enter the name you want to give the report and click the Finish button.

In our example, the subdatasheet displays the record of the supplier linked to the article. Click on the plus sign in front of the supplier (it will turn into a minus sign) and a new subdatasheet will be displayed containing all the articles that the supplier carries.

You can edit the data of the table displayed in the subdatasheet exactly as you do for the main datasheet.

Click the minus sign to close the lower subdatasheet. To open or close the subdatasheets of all the records of the table, select the Format/Datasheet/Expand All or Collapse All.

The Format/Subdatasheet/Remove command will cancel the sub-datasheet: the column of small plus signs will disappear.

If you make an error when choosing linked fields (parent and child), *Access* displays a message indicating that there is no relationship between the two fields and will offer to establish the relationship for you. Let *Access* do so, since you will have to return to this dialogue box.

ARTICLES : Table

	Code	Name	Category	Supplier	Pric
+	25-070	Red document box (per hundred)	Stationery	5	
+	25-071	Blue document box (per hundred)	Stationery	5	
+	25-072	Yellow document box (per hundred)	Stationery	5	
▶ −	25-073	Black document box (per hundred)	Stationery	5	

	Co	Company	Address	Post Code	City
▶ −	5	Alpha plus	17 Picpus Street	MA2 9JB	Manches

	Code	Name	Category	P
▶ +	25-069	Green document box (per hundred)	Stationery	
+	25-070	Red document box (per hundred)	Stationery	
+	25-071	Blue document box (per hundred)	Stationery	
+	25-072	Yellow document box (per hundred)	Stationery	
+	25-073	Black document box (per hundred)	Stationery	
+	25-074	Grey document box (per hundred)	Stationery	
+	25-075	Brown document box (per hundred)	Stationery	

Record: 14 ◀ 1 ▶ ▶I ▶* of 14

Tools/Relationships

56

57

Datasheet

Subdatasheet

If several tables are related in your database, you can show the linked records in the datasheet. Select the Insert/Subdatasheet command. In the list, select the table whose data you want to see.

Then select the child field (the field of the subtable used to link the two tables). Finally, select the parent field (the link field in the table displayed in the datasheet).

In our example, the Articles table is displayed in the datasheet and the Suppliers table was chosen for the subdatasheet. The child field is Number (in the Suppliers table) and the parent field is Suppliers (in the Articles table).

Back in the datasheet, you will note an additional column in the left pane: it contains a box with a plus sign. Click this plus sign to view the subfield.

Syntax and operators by field type

Text fields

="text"	Contains exactly "text".
<>"text"	Does not contain "text".
Like "*text*"	Contains "text" anywhere in the field.

Three wildcard characters are recognised with the Like operator:

* replaces an indefinite number of any characters.

? replaces a single character.

replaces a single number.

<	Less than.
>	Greater than.
<=	Less than or equal to.
>=	Greater than or equal to.
Is Null	Empty.
Is Not Null	Not empty.
Not "text"	Does not contain "text".
"text1" or "text2"	Contains "text1" or "text2".

Record/Filters

Number fields

=158	Contains exactly 158.
<>158	Does not contain 158.
>158	Contains a value greater than 158.
<158	Contains a value less than 158.
>=158	Contains a value greater than or equal to 158.
<=158	Contains a value less than or equal to 158.
Between 158 and 197	Contains a value between 158 and 197 (equivalent to >=158 And <=197).
Is Null	Empty.
Is Not Null	Not empty.
Not 158	Does not contain 158.
158 or 297	Contains 158 or 297.

Dates fields

Use the same operators as for number fields by framing a date with a hash mark (#), e.g.

<#15/2/2000#	Before 15 February 2000.
Between #10/12/1999# And #15/2/2000#	Between 10 December 1999 and 15 February 2000.

58

Select queries

When you create a new query, it is a select query by default. The type of query is displayed in the title of its window.

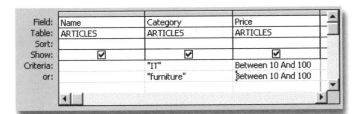

Drag into the grid the fields to be displayed in the datasheet and those for which you want to define filter criteria.

Enter the select criteria. All the criteria on the top row are interlinked with the logical operator AND (all the criteria must be true for a record to be selected).

The different rows of criteria beneath are interlinked by the logical operator OR.

In the example on the right, the query must display records whose Categories field contains 'information technology' or 'furniture' and whose Price field contains a value between 10 and 100.

Name	Category	Price
Guest chair	Furniture	40
Round Table	Furniture	61
Low sectional unit	Furniture	48
Large black desk	Furniture	67
Secretarial desk	Furniture	97
Small desk	Furniture	63
Mobile three-drawer filing cabinet	Furniture	81
Printer stand	Furniture	46
Digital cartridges DC6320	IT	12
Digital cartridges DC6525	IT	14

! Run

□ Show Table...

Remove Table

➤ Select Query

Crosstab Query

! Make-Table Query...

! Update Query

! Append Query...

! Delete Query

SQL Specific

Parameters...

Query/Select Query

Ready

NUM

An expression may contain field names, operators, constants and functions supplied by *Access*.

Constants

Text data must be framed by ":	"information technology".
Date data must be framed by #:	#12/3/2000#.
Numerical data is not framed:	12552.
Field names are framed by square brackets:	[label].

Some mathematical functions

Int	Integer.	Abs	Absolute value.
Rnd	Rounded off.		

Some date functions

Now	Current date and time.	Year	Year.
Weekday	Day of the week.	Day	Day of the month.
Month	Month.		

Some text functions

Left	Extract characters from the left.
Right	Extract characters from the right.
UCase	Convert to uppercase.
Len	Number of characters.

Query2 : Select Query

Name	Price included VAT
Half-height unit	161
Low sectional unit	57
Executive desk	129
Large black desk	80
Secretarial desk	116
Small desk	75
Mobile three-drawer filing cabinet	97
Printer stand	55
Green document box (per hundred)	13
Red document box (per hundred)	13
Blue document box (per hundred)	13
Yellow document box (per hundred)	13
Black document box (per hundred)	13
Grey document box (per hundred)	13
Brown document box (per hundred)	13
Fax 7	66
3.5" diskette	2
CD-Rom	2

Record: 1 of 41

The datasheet displays the result of the calculated field and the data of the fields whose View checkbox was ticked in the query grid.

Insert/Table

60

Calculated fields

As you know, it makes no sense to introduce to the structure of a table fields whose contents depend on the contents of another field. For example, in the Articles table, a Price inclusive of all tax field would depend on the contents of the Price and VAT fields. As it is impossible to insert a calculated field in a table, you must do this in a query.

In the query design grid, click the first empty cell of the top row (where the names of the fields are displayed). Type directly the expression to be calculated and open the Expression Builder window: click with the right button in the empty cell and select the Build command. The expression is built in the upper area. The folders in the lower left pane contain the elements available for creating the expression. To insert an element in the expression, double-click its name. You can also type the data on the keyboard.

When the expression is built, click OK. By default, the calculated field is called Expr1: change the name, but leave the colon that separates it from the expression.

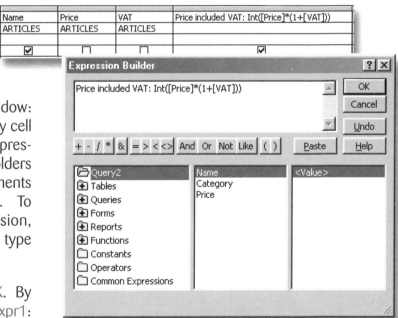

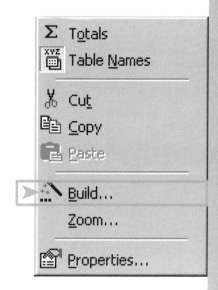

If you save the query, its name (accompanied by a specific icon) will appear in the Database window. Double-click this icon: an initial message will appear telling you that you are going to run an update query command and that the data will be modified.

Warning: an update will be carried out every time you run this query. In our example, the current price is multiplied by 1.1 every time the query is run.

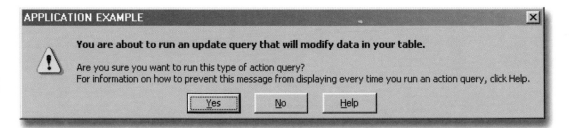

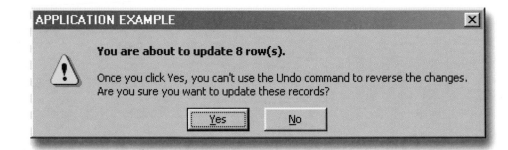

Some examples

- Convert the contents of the Name field to uppercase: UCase ([Name])
- Round off prices to the first decimal: Rnd ([Price];1)
- In an invoice table, enter Yes or No in the Reminder field depending on whether the invoice is older than 30 days: Iif ([Date]+30<Now();"yes"; "no")

View/Datasheet View

Access: Query / Update Query

Query design

Modify data by a query

You can always edit the data manually in the datasheet of course, but when you have to, say, increase the price of all the information technology articles by 10%, this becomes tedious. An Update query can carry out the changes rapidly and free of errors.

Select the Query/ Update Query command. The window title displays the type of query: Update Query. An additional row entitled Update To is inserted in the query grid.

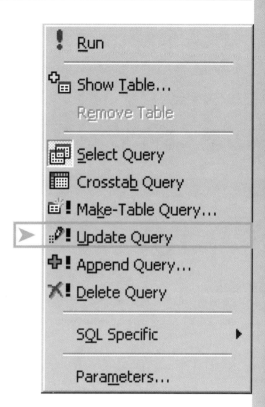

Field:	Name	Category	Price	Supplier	
Table:	ARTICLES	ARTICLES	ARTICLES	ARTICLES	
Update To:			[Price]*1.1		
Criteria:		"IT"			
or:					

Drag into the grid the fields on which you have to apply a filter as well as those whose contents will be modified. Enter the filter criteria as for a select query. Then click in the Update To row of the column of the field containing the data to be modified. Enter the expression whose result will replace the field data. In our example, the contents of the Price field will be replaced by the result Int([Price]*1.1): the price is multiplied by 1.1 and only the integer (whole number) is kept.

To run this query, select the Query/Run command or click the Run button. The data will be modified immediately without any possibility of cancellation.

Query / Update Query

Ready

NUM

Confirmation messages

If you save the query, its name, accompanied by a specific icon, will appear in the Database window. Double-click on this icon: an initial message will appear telling you that you are going to run a delete query command that will modify (delete) data.

If you are not too sure of yourself, make a copy of the table before you apply the delete query. If everything goes the way you want, you can just delete the copy.

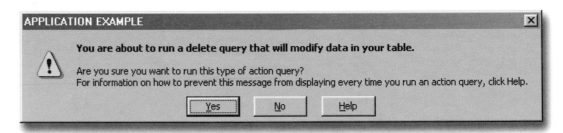

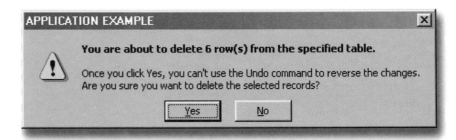

Some examples

- To delete last year's invoices, enter the following expression in the invoice date field column: Year([date of invoice])<Year(Now())
- To delete from a contacts table those who do not have an email address, enter the following expressing in the Address field: Is Null

View/Datasheet View

64

65

Delete records by query

A Delete Query deletes records rapidly and free of errors.

Select the Query/Delete Query command. The window title displays the type of query: Delete Query. An additional row entitled Delete is inserted in the query grid.

Drag into the grid the fields to which you want to apply a filter. In this type of query, the records corresponding to the filter criteria will be deleted. Enter the filter criteria as in a select query.

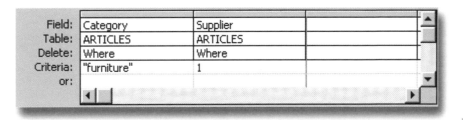

Field:	Category	Supplier	
Table:	ARTICLES	ARTICLES	
Delete:	Where	Where	
Criteria:	"furniture"	1	
or:			

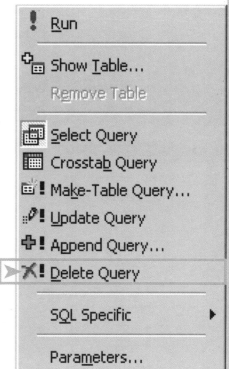

- ! Run
- ⊞ Show Table...
- Remove Table
- ▦ Select Query
- ▦ Crosstab Query
- ▦! Make-Table Query...
- ▱! Update Query
- ➕! Append Query...
- ✕! Delete Query
- SQL Specific ▶
- Parameters...

To run this query, select Query/Run or click the Run button. A message will inform you that you are going to delete a certain number of rows (i.e. records). Click Yes to run the query. The data will be deleted immediately without any possibility of cancellation.

As a precaution, make a select query by applying the filter you have created. You will then see the list of records selected by the filter. Once you have checked this list, you can transform the select query into a delete query to delete the records.

Query/Delete Query

NUM

Some tips

If you leave the parameters area empty in the dialogue box, no record will be displayed in the datasheet. To get all the records of the table when the setting is left empty, the filter criterion to enter is the expression:

Like [Which category ?] & "*"

The default parameter is text. If you want it to be recognised as date or number data, you must declare it accordingly.

Select the Query/Parameters command to open the Query Parameters window. Enter the name of the setting as you typed it in the criteria box, and select the data type in the left column.

If you delete or modify the parameter in the query grid, do the same in the Query Parameters window.

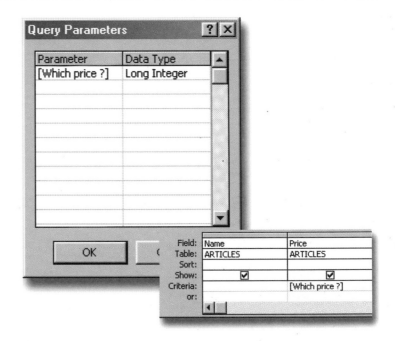

Records/Filter

Access: Query/Parameters

Set a query

In a query, the filter criteria are set in the grid. To modify the filter, you must necessarily open the query in Design View unless you set the query.

In such a case, when you run the query, a dialogue box will appear where you can enter data to serve as filter criteria. In the example on the right, the article category entered in the Enter Parameter Value box (here, furniture) is used as a criterion to filter the table.

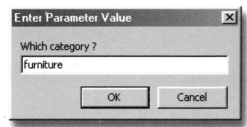

In the query grid, enter the filter criterion normally and replace the constant by the name of the setting. Here, instead of the 'furniture' constant, enter '[Which category?]' as your criterion. When the query is run, a Parameters dialogue box will appear. The data you enter in it will replace the parameter in the expression used as a filter criterion.

In our example, ['[Which category?]' is automatically replaced in the query by 'furniture'. This replacement is temporary: the next time the query is run, you can enter, for instance, 'information technology' or 'stationery' as a setting.

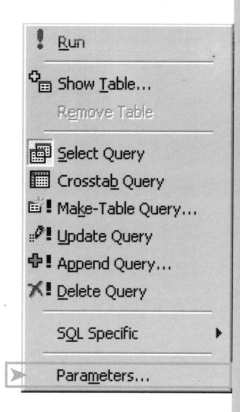

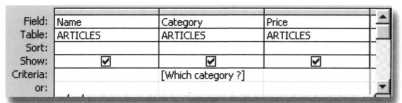

Field:	Name	Category	Price	
Table:	ARTICLES	ARTICLES	ARTICLES	
Sort:				
Show:	☑	☑	☑	
Criteria:		[Which category ?]		
or:				

Ready   NUM

Characters and cell size

In addition to the overall appearance of the datasheet, you can also apply a font, a font size and colour. Select the Format/Font command. In the dialogue box, select a Font, a Font Style, Size and Color. Click OK. Your selection will be applied to all the data of the datasheet, including the column headers. It is impossible to change the appearance of only a few fields in the datasheet. You must use a form for this purpose.

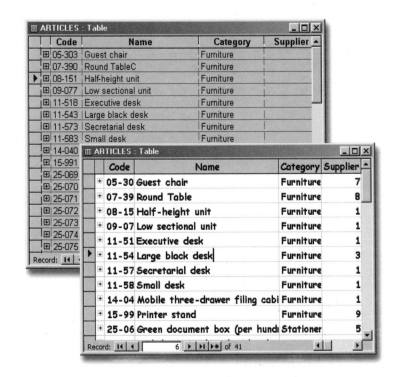

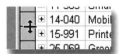

To change the row height, point in the left column on the line between two rows and drag the mouse. All the rows of the datasheet always have the same height.

To change the column width, point to the right border of the column header and drag the mouse.

Format/Row height - Column Width

68

69

Access: Format/Datasheet

Datasheet formatting

You don't have to keep the default white background. The Format/Datasheet command opens a dialogue box in which you can change the overall appearance of the datasheet.

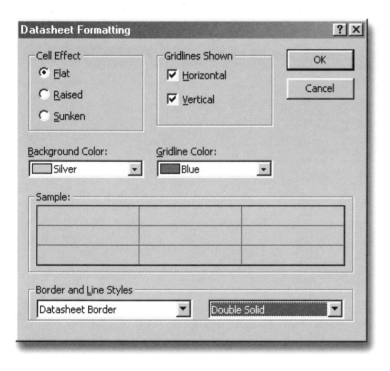

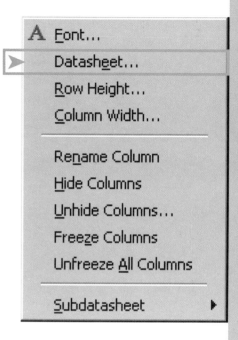

Select the Cell Effect: two dimensions (Flat) or three dimensions (Raised or Sunken). If you choose Flat, you can also set the Background Color and the Gridline Color. In the Border and Line Styles list, you have access to four types of lines (Datasheet Border, Horizontal Gridline, Vertical Gridline and Column Header Underline). Select the one you want, then select a line style from the list on the right. When you click OK, the datasheet will be displayed according to the chosen settings.

When you close the datasheet, a message will ask you whether you want to save the formatting changes. Click Yes if you want to save the new datasheet settings.

To move a column, you must select it first. Point above its header (the cursor turns into a black arrow) and click. Click in the header, keep the mouse button pressed, and drag the mouse horizontally. This operation has no effect on the structure of the table.

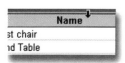

When a table contains too many fields, they cannot all be shown on the screen. You can scroll the window to the right to view the subsequent fields. Fields that must remain displayed at all times on the left side of the screen (article headings, for instance) can be frozen. Click anywhere in the column you want to freeze and select the Format/Freeze Columns command. The column is automatically moved to the far left and the window scrolls through all the others. You can thus freeze several columns. A thicker vertical line marks the divide between the two parts of the window. To unfreeze the columns, you can select the Unfreeze All Columns command.

	Code	Name	Category	Supplier	
+	05-303	Guest chair	Furniture	7	
▶ +	07-390	Round Table	Furniture	8	
+	08-151	Half-height unit	Furniture	1	
+	09-077	Low sectional unit	Furniture	1	
+	11-518	Executive desk	Furniture	1	
+	11-543	Large black desk	Furniture	3	
+	11-573	Secretarial desk	Furniture	1	
+	11-583	Small desk	Furniture	1	
+	14-040	Mobile three-drawer filing cabinet	Furniture	1	
+	15-991	Printer stand	Furniture	9	
+	25-069	Green document box (per hundred)	Stationery	5	
+	25-070	Red document box (per hundred)	Stationery	5	
+	25-071	Blue document box (per hundred)	Stationery	5	
+	25-072	Yellow document box (per hundred)	Stationery	5	

ARTICLES : Table

Record: 2 of 41

View/Design View

70
71

Playing with columns

A number of commands in the Format menu pertain to columns.

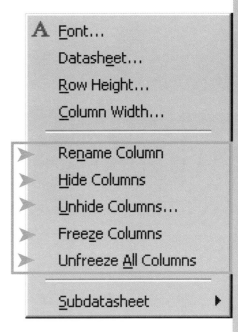

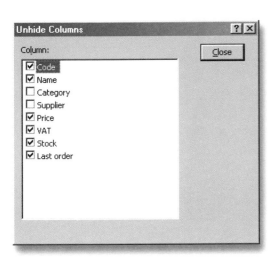

The Rename Column command is dangerous, for the column name corresponds to the name of the field and changing it is tantamount to renaming the field in the Create Table window. It is better to rename the fields in the Design View because all the objects that include this field (forms, queries, reports) must be updated.

To hide a column, click in any cell of the column and select the Format/Hide Columns command. Only the necessary data will then be kept on the screen. To display the hidden columns again, select Format/Unhide Columns. Tick the column headers you wish to display.

Bear in mind that *Access* prints the datasheet exactly as it is displayed. Hidden columns, for example, are not printed.

Overlays

It is possible to group the selected controls to form a single object by selecting the Format/Group command. You can ungroup them with Format/Ungroup.

Each control in the form is situated in an invisible, transparent layer. The different overlays are, as their name implies, overlaid. As long as the controls are not covered, there is no problem. However, as soon as they are covered, the object situated on the upper overlay hides (totally or partially) those underneath. The Format/ Bring To Front command brings the selected overlay to the front of all the others, whereas the Format/Send To Back puts the selected control to the back of all the others.

The form is framed by a 'magnetised' grid that helps you position the controls. This grid can be displayed or hidden with the View/Grid command. You can align the selected controls to the grid with the Format/Align/To Grid command.

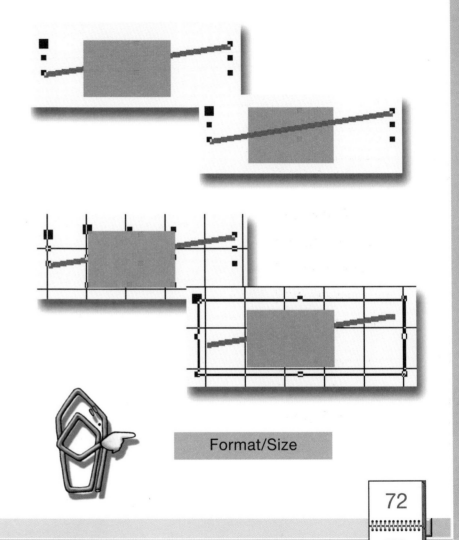

Format/Size

Access: Format/Align

Handling the controls

When creating a form, the formatting of the controls (their size, alignment in relation to each other, etc.) is the most time-consuming task. The Format menu features several commands that will make it easier to manage controls.

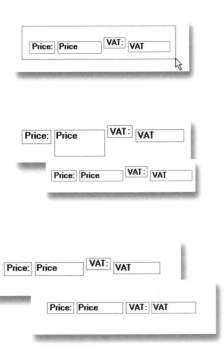

To select several controls, frame them with the cursor. Alternatively, keep the Shift key pressed and click on the different controls.

Attribute the same size to all the selected controls: choose the Format/Size command and then click on To Tallest, for example, so that they are all given the largest height.

Align the selected controls: select the Format/Align command and click Bottom, for example.

Adjust their horizontal and vertical spacing automatically by selecting the Format/Horizontal Spacing or Format/Vertical Spacing.

Design View

NUM

In the filter form window, you can delete all the conditions by clicking the Clear Grid button.

A filter is essentially a rapid query and you can save it as such using the File/Save As Query command. It will be used, along with the other queries, in the database window. Conversely, you can import an existing query into the form with the File/Load from Query.

When a filter is active in a datasheet, the button filter is pressed and *Access* indicates the number of displayed records in the lower left corner of the window.

As the current filter is kept (and saved) with the datasheet, you can activate or deactivate the filter at all times by clicking the filter button in the toolbar. You will find the criteria of the current filter simply by clicking Filter by Form button or the Records/Filter/ Filter by Form command.

Operators for filter criteria

=	Equal to.	<>	Other than.
>	Greater than.	<	Less than.
>=	Greater than or equal to.	<=	Less than or equal to.

Is Null   Empty field.
Is not Null   Not empty field.

And   Logical AND.   Or   Logical OR.
Not   Logical NOT.

Text data is put between double quotation marks ("..").
Date data is put between hash marks (#...#).

Samples

<>"book">#1/2/2000#
>50 And <=120 >#1/3/2000# And <31/3/2000#

There is no differentiation between upper- and lowercase.

Insert/Query

Filter by Form

When you filter a table, only the records corresponding to the filter criteria remain visible. The others are not deleted but simply hidden. To filter a table, select the Records/Filter/Filter by Form.

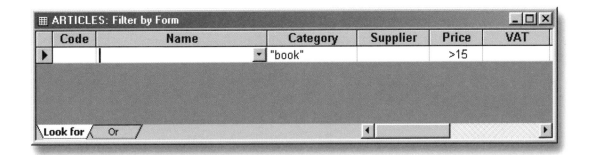

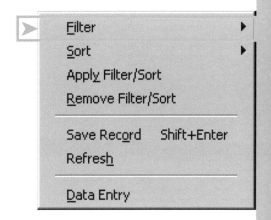

Filter	▶
Sort	▶
Apply Filter/Sort	
Remove Filter/Sort	
Save Record	Shift+Enter
Refresh	
Data Entry	

The form that opens contains a single row in which you enter the filter conditions. All the criteria in a form page are linked by the logical operator AND. In our example, when the filter is activated, Access will apply it to each record and will display only those whose Category field contains 'book' and whose Price field contains a value greater than 15.

Record/Filter/Filter by Form

If you want to view the articles of the 'book' and 'information technology' categories, these two criteria must be linked by the logical operator OR. Access will then pick the records in which the Category field contains 'book' or 'information technology'. Enter 'book' in the Category column and click the Or tab to type 'information technology' in the Category column on the second page of the form. Click the Apply Filter button to activate the filter.

Once defined, the Filter by Selection or Filter Excluding Selection is saved in the form. Select the Records/Filter/Filter by Form command or click the button of the same name and you will find the selection condition.

In our example, the selection of a word inside a field is translated in the form by the Like operator, making it possible to introduce asterisks (*) and question marks (?) in the expression, where:

  * replaces any number of characters and

  ? replaces a single character.

For example, Like "*video*" means that the filter will search all records whosecurrent field contains in particular the word "video", without distinction between upper- and lowercase.

When you close the datasheet, Access will suggest saving the changes made to the structure of the table. Click the Yes button if you want to keep the current filter. You can then apply it next time you open the datasheet.

Filter by form, by selection or by query: Which one to choose ?

	Filter by and excluding selection	Filter by form	Query
Logical OR	No	Yes	Yes
Logical AND	No	Yes	Yes
Comparison operators	No	Yes	Yes
Filter and sort	No	No	Yes

ARTICLES: Filter by Form — □ ×

Code	Name	Category	Supplier	Pri
▶	Like "*desk" ▼			

Look for / Or /

Insert/Query

76

77

Datasheet

Filter by Selection

The Filter by Selection command is faster but less sophisticated than the Filter by Form command.

Select an entire field or some of the data it contains. Choose the Records/Filter/Filter by Selection command. *Access* will immediately display the records whose active field contains the selected data. The number of filtered records is displayed in the lower left corner of the window. You can also reverse the filter by asking to view the records whose active field does not contain the selected data. In such a case, select Records/Filter/Filter Excluding Selection.

To disable the filter, select Records/Show All Records or click the Remove filter button.

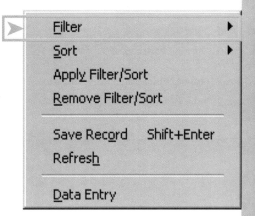

Filter	▶
Sort	▶
Apply Filter/Sort	
Remove Filter/Sort	
Save Record	Shift+Enter
Refresh	
Data Entry	

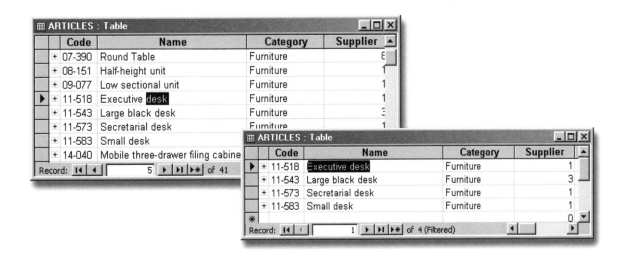

Record/Filter/
Filter by Selection

Sort text or numbers

Access sorts according to the field data type used as a criterion: alphabetically in a text field, numerically in a number field or chrono-logically in a date field.

If a text field contains the data 5, 36, 12, 114, they will be sorted in the order 114, 12, 36, 5, because the character 1 is situated before the character 2, etc. If the same digits are in a number field, they will be sorted in the order of their value: 5, 12, 36, 114.

Special characters (ç for example) will be sorted at the appropriate letter ('c') provided that the sort type is set correctly for that langua-ge. Select (in this case) the Tools/Options command and click the General tab. In the New Database Sort Order list, select the data language in the tables.

When you close the datasheet, *Access* will ask you to save the changes made to the structure of the table. Click Yes if you want the data to be sorted automatically next time you open the datasheet.

ARTICLES : Table			
Code	Category	Name	
▶ 31-081	Audiovisual	Audio micro cassettes	
31-086	Audiovisual	Office electronic diary	
31-082	Audiovisual	Office Playback device	
31-087	Audiovisual	Pocket electronic diary	
31-084	Audiovisual	Pocket memo	
31-085	Audiovisual	Professional pocket memo	
31-080	Audiovisual	Standard audio cassettes	
78-996	Communication	'Wireless' Intercom - 2 sets	
78-997	Communication	'Wireless' Intercom - 3 sets	
25-663	Communication	Fax 7	
75-632	Communication	Fax cleaning kit	
85-669	Communication	Minitel Printer	
11-518	Furniture	Executive desk	
05-303	Furniture	Guest chair	
08-151	Furniture	Half-height unit	
11-543	Furniture	Large black desk	
34-824	Furniture	Leather executive armchair	
09-077	Furniture	Low sectional unit	
14-040	Furniture	Mobile three-drawer filing cabinet	
34-821	Furniture	Plush executive armchair	
15-991	Furniture	Printer stand	

Record: I◀ ◀ 1 ▶ ▶I ▶* of 40

The table after sorting the Category and Name fields

Insert/Query

Datasheet

Sort records

When you sort a table, all the records are kept but arranged in a specific order.

To sort the contents of a field, click in the field (in any record) and then select the Records/Sort command, and click one of the two buttons (Sort Ascending or Sort Descending).

To sort several fields, first move the columns to arrange them one after the other. Point above the header of the column you want to move: when the cursor turns into a black arrow, click and then drag the column to its new location.

When all the columns that will serve as a sorting criterion are in the correct order, select them: point above the header of the first column and when the black arrow appears, click and drag the mouse on the neighbouring columns. Then run the sort command in the Records menu or by clicking one of the two buttons.

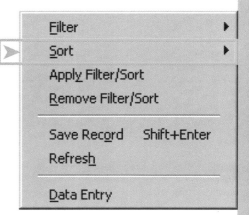

Code	Category	Name
05-303	Furniture	Guest chair
07-390	Furniture	Round Table
08-151	Furniture	Half-height unit
09-077	Furniture	Low sectional unit
11-518	Furniture	Executive desk
11-543	Furniture	Large black desk
11-573	Furniture	Secretarial desk
11-583	Furniture	Small desk
14-040	Furniture	Mobile three-drawer filing cabinet
15-991	Furniture	Printer stand
25-069	Stationery	Green document box (per hundred)
25-070	Stationery	Red document box (per hundred)
25-071	Stationery	Blue document box (per hundred)
25-072	Stationery	Yellow document box (per hundred)
25-073	Stationery	Black document box (per hundred)
25-074	Stationery	Grey document box (per hundred)
25-075	Stationery	Brown document box (per hundred)
25-663	Communication	Fax 7
31-068	IT	3.5" diskette
31-070	IT	CD-Rom
31-072	IT	Digital cartridges DC300 XL/P

Record: 1 of 41

Record/Sort

Filter
Sort
Apply Filter/Sort
Remove Filter/Sort
Save Record   Shift+Enter
Refresh
Data Entry

Word document

Type the letter as you would normally. When you want to enter data from the Access table, click the Insert Merge Field button and select the field you want from the list. When you have finished your letter, save it and test it. Click the MailMerge button and then use the arrows to scroll the records. The contents of the inserted fields are displayed in plain text.

Finally click the Merge button. The dialogue box indicates that the merge result will be transferred to a new document, not directly to the printer. If you retain this option, you can see the result one last time before printing the document.

If you have saved the standard letter, it can be used for the next merge. In the first Wizard dialogue box, tick the Link the data to an existing Word document box to select the standard letter document.

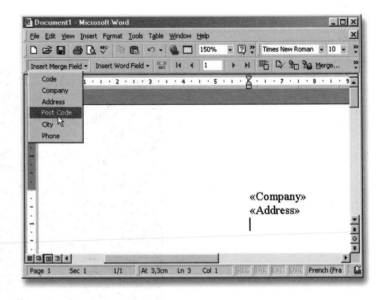

Insert/Report

Access: Tools/Office links

Database

Merge with Word

There is nothing like *Word* for printing labels, envelopes or letters with the data of a table. A Wizard will guide you on how to merge *Access* with *Word*. Select the table or query that you want to merge. You can also open the datasheet of the table and apply a filter as and when necessary. Bear in mind that it is not possible to merge with a form or report.

Then open the command Tools/ Office Links/Merge It with MS Word. The Wizard will ask you if you want to link your data to an existing *Word* document or to create a new document (a standard letter or page of labels prepared in advance). Let us take the example of a new document. When you click OK, *Word* opens a blank document already associated to the *Access* table. You can then proceed by selecting the Tools/Mail Merge command in *Word*.

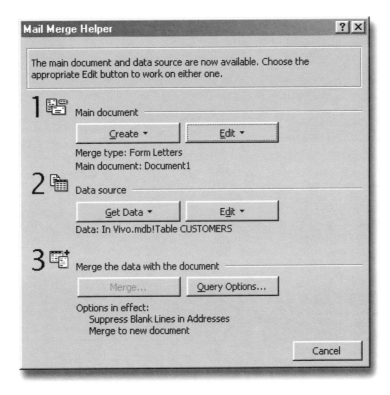

Ready

NUM

Exporting to *Word* works in exactly the same way. Select the table or query and click Tools/Office Links/Publish it with MS Word. A *Word* document will then open containing the data in table form, without keeping the link with the *Access* table.

Whether transferring to *Word* or *Excel*, the command exports the data exactly as it appears in the datasheet. The data and character formatting are retained. If a filter is applied, only the visible data is transferred in the order of the active sorting. And if columns are hidden, they will not be appear in the *Word* or *Excel* table.

Conversely, the File/Export command saves the entire table in Excel, Word, Lotus, Paradox, dBase or text only, without taking account of the formatting, hidden columns or current filter or sorting.

To create a link to an *Access* table from *Word* or *Excel*, you must use the Insert command of an OLE object and tick the Link option.

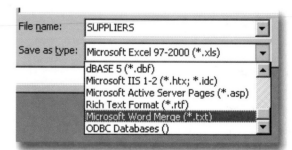

	A	B	C	D	E
1	Code	Company	Address	Post Code	City
2	1	Buro	121 South Molton Street	W1Y 1HY	London
3	2	RapidService	128 East Street	PO16 9XE	Portchester
4	3	XLStore	4 Stroud Road	GL1 4JE	Gloucester
5	4	Centre Red	15 Blackwater Church Road	E4F 2JH	London
6	5	Alpha plus	17 Picpus Street	MA2 9JB	Manchester
7	6	Martin Company	4523 Blalock Road	N5K 8LP	London
8	7	Enterprise Edition	7 Smith Brewer Road	MA2 3BF	Manchester
9	8	Audio Max	108 Pearl Street	CA3 8AC	Canterbury
10	9	Info Media	5 Houser Road	W3G 5GC	London
11	10	Modern Style	885 Station Street	MA5 7CD	Manchester

File name: SUPPLIERS

Save as type: Microsoft Excel 97-2000 (*.xls)

dBASE 5 (*.dbf)
Microsoft IIS 1-2 (*.htx; *.idc)
Microsoft Active Server Pages (*.asp)
Rich Text Format (*.rtf)
Microsoft Word Merge (*.txt)
ODBC Databases ()

File/Export

Export to Excel and Word

Access is adept at managing tables, adding, deleting, finding and, above all, linking data. It is rather weak, however, at calculations and graphics. *Excel*, on the other hand, is the opposite. The two software applications complement each other perfectly and the data from an *Access* table can be transferred to an *Excel* spreadsheet.

	A	B	C	D	E
1	Code	Company	Address	Post Code	City
2	1	Buro	121 South Molton Street	W1Y 1HY	London
3	2	RapidService	128 East Street	PO16 9XE	Portchester
4	3	XLStore	4 Stroud Road	GL1 4JE	Gloucester
5	4	Center Red	15 Blackwater Church Road	E4F 2JH	London
6	5	Alpha plus	17 Picpus Street	MA2 9JB	Manchester
7	6	Martin Company	4523 Blalock Road	N5K 8LP	London
8	7	Enterprise Edition	7 Smith Brewer Road	MA2 3BF	Manchester
9	8	Audio Max	108 Pearl Street	CA3 8AC	Canterbury
10	9	Info Media	5 Houser Road	W3G 5GC	London
11	10	Modern Style	885 Station Street	MA5 7CD	Manchester

SUPPLIERS.xls — SUPPLIERS

Select the table or query and then click Tools/Office Links/Analyze It with MS Excel. After a few seconds, Excel will open a spreadsheet containing the data of the table. However, contrary to what the name of the command suggests, there is no link between the spreadsheet and the table. The changes in one will not be transferred to the other.

You can do the same from a form or a report, but the result is less satisfactory and, in most cases, unusable.

Spelling... — F7
AutoCorrect...
Office Links
Online Collaboration
Relationships...
Analyze
Database Utilities
Security
Replication
Startup...
Macro
ActiveX Controls...
Add-Ins
Customize...
Options...

Referential integrity

The Edit Relationships dialogue box opens when a relationship is created, or when you double-click the join line between two or more tables.

To lock the relationship between the two tables, tick Enforce Referential Integrity to refuse any orphan record in the child table. For example, a record in the Articles child table is an orphan if it contains the number 25 in its Supplier field, since no record in the Suppliers (parent) table contains the value 25 in its Number field.

Referential integrity prevents any deletion of a record in the parent table if there are no corresponding records in the child table, unless the Cascade Delete Related Records is ticked.

Referential integrity prevents any editing of the contents of the primary key field in the parent table, unless the Cascade Update Related Fields option is ticked.

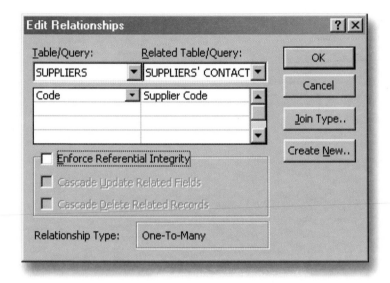

Tools/Analyze

84

85

Create relationships between tables

To create a relationship between tables, the parent table must contain a primary key field. The child table must contain a field of the same type and size as the primary key in the parent table. See the more detailed explanatory remarks in the introduction for more information.

In the window opened by selecting Tools/ Relationships, display the tables you want to relate with the Show Table/Add Table command. The small windows show the list of fields (with the primary key in bold). Move and resize these windows to suit your needs.

To create a relationship between two tables, click the primary key field in the parent table and drag it to the relevant field in the child table. When you release the mouse, the Edit Relationships dialogue box opens. Simply click the Create button. To delete a relationship, click on the line (displayed in bold) and press the Del key.

When you close the relationships window, a dialogue box will ask you whether you wish to save the changes. Clicking Yes or No makes no difference to the relationships you have created: the window concerns only the displayed elements and their layout in the relationships window.

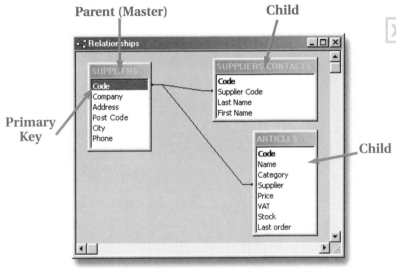

Tools/Relationships

Analyse performance

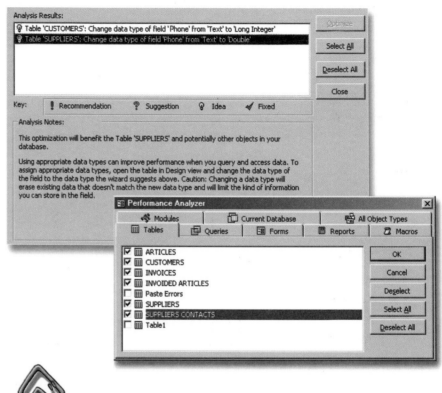

Access uses the Tools/Analyze/Performance command to analyse objects you have selected beforehand, and displays its results and solutions a few seconds later.

Select one of the problems detected from the list. A full explanation is provided in the Analysis Notes at the bottom of the window. If a suggestion or recommendation is offered, click the Optimize button to have *Access* carry out the adjustment. The problems solved are preceded by the Fixed mark. Remember that *Access* cannot carry out adjustments for ideas: this is something you have to do yourself once you have closed the Performance Analyzer.

The third command (Tools/Analyze/Documenter) helps you create the document folder for your database. In the Preview window, it displays the description pages of objects you have selected. Use the Options button to choose the elements you want to include in this description. All you have to do then is print the result.

Tools/Relationships

Analyse a database

A relational database must observe certain rules (see p.6). One of these rules stipulates that a data item can be found only in one location (in a single field or a single record of a single table). The Table Analyzer detects duplicates and, when it finds any, breaks down the table to create a system of relationships between the new tables it proposes. In any event, the original table is kept.

Select the Tools/Analyze/Table command. The first two screens explain how the Table Analyzer works. In the third, select the table to be analysed. Leave Yes, Let the Wizard Decide ticked, so that the Wizard can do just that. In the next screen, the Wizard will offer to create a query that groups all the fields of all the tables.

You must take up the Wizard's proposal. Move the fields between the tables (one empty table will disappear automatically). If you move a field outside of any table, a new table will be created. When the tables are built properly, click on the button in the upper right-hand corner of this window to name them. In the next screen, the Wizard will prompt you to create a query grouping all the fields of all the tables.

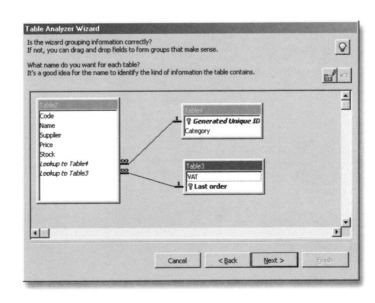

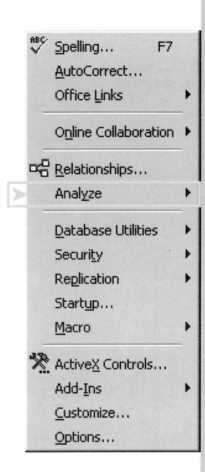

When you untick the Allow Default Shortcut Menus, no menu normally opened with the right mouse button will be available.

Select from the Display Form/Page the form that will open automatically when you start the database.

Untick the Display Database Window so that it is hidden. To make it reappear, press the F11 key. To block the use of this F11 key, click the Advanced button and untick the Use Access Special Keys option.

The status bar can remain hidden (Display Status Bar option) as well as the toolbars (Allow Built-In Toolbars). If you do not allow toolbar changes, you preclude the possibility of adding or removing buttons.

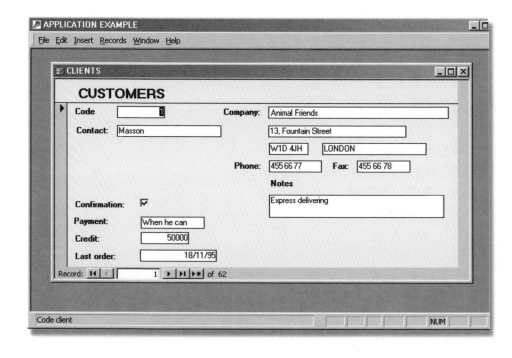

Compact and repair database

As you add and remove records, empty spaces are interspersed in the database, increasing the size of the file to no purpose and slowing down database operation. Furthermore, a database is modified and becomes unusable. Databases can be compacted and repaired with the command: Tools/Database Utilities/Compact and Repair Databases. This command works on the open database or any database you have selected.

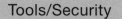

Set the database Startup

When you open the database, the Database window is displayed by default. All the menus and objects are available. Nevertheless, you can, without having to program anything, set the Startup to open a form auto-matically and hide the Database window, for example.

Search the hard disk for an icon file

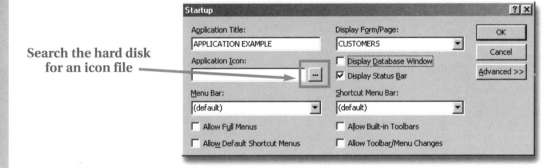

The Startup dialogue box offers various options for customising how the database opens.

The Application Title will be displayed in the Access window title bar.

The Application Icon will be associated with the database file rather than with the standard Access icon. Click the triple-dot button to search the hard disk for an icon file (extension .ico) which must be 32 x 32 dots in size.

If you have programmed a personal menu bar, it will be included in the list.

If you untick the Allow Full Menus option, a minimal tool bar will be available. It will contain only the File/Exit, File/Close and the Window and ? (Help) menus.

Settings

When you click on the AutoCorrect button, you can enter words that you frequently misspell and suggest replacement words (in the Change To field). Each time you type the wrong word, it will be replaced automatically by the correct word. The AutoCorrect list is available through the Tools/AutoCorrect command.

The custom dictionary and the default list of corrections are shared by all *Office* applications.

When you click on the Options button, you can set the spelling checker to prevent it from, for example, stopping on words in capitals or on words composed of a set of letters and numbers. In the same dialogue box, you can select the language of the main dictionary. Untick the option From Main Dictionary Only if you want the spelling checker to check the words with the language dictionary *and* the custom dictionary.

Warning

Spelling corrections are entered immediately and irreversibly in the fields. They cannot be cancelled.

Tools/AutoCorrect

Access: Tools/Spelling

Check the spelling

Select the fields or an entire table to be checked, then select the Tools/Spelling command.

The spelling checker will stop on each word contained neither in the language dictionary nor the custom dictionary.

For each of the words on which the spelling checker stops, select the appropriate action:

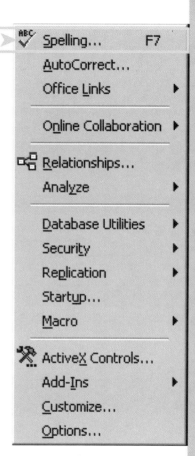

- **Ignore**: The spelling checker moves on to the next word without changing anything.

- **Ignore All**: The spelling checker will no longer stop on this word if it appears subsequently.

- **Change**: The word is replaced by the one in the Change To field.

- **Change All**: The word will be replaced automatically everywhere it occurs.

- **Add**: The word is added to the custom dictionary selected in the Add Words To list.

- **Undo Last**: Cancels the previous correction.

NUM

Thematic index

NUM

Access: Index

Ready NUM